总 策 划：许　琳

总 监 制：静　炜　王君校

监　　制：夏建辉　韩　晖　张彤辉　刘　研

主　　编：吴中伟

编　　者：吴中伟　吴叔平　高顺全　吴金利

修　　订：吴中伟

顾　　问：陶黎铭　陈光磊

Dāngdài Zhōngwén

当代中文
修订版

Contemporary Chinese
Revised Edition

Hànzìběn

汉字本
1
CHARACTER BOOK
Volume One

主　编：吴中伟

编　者：吴中伟　吴叔平

　　　　高顺全　吴金利

翻　译：徐　蔚

　　　　Yvonne L. Walls　Jan W. Walls

译文审校：Jerry Schmidt

Sinolingua
华语教学出版社

First Edition 2003

Revised Edition 2014

Sixth Printing 2020

ISBN 978-7-5138-0619-0

Copyright 2014 by Sinolingua Co., Ltd

Published by Sinolingua Co., Ltd

24 Baiwanzhuang Street, Beijing 100037, China

Tel: (86)10-68320585, 68997826

Fax: (86)10-68997826, 68326333

http://www.sinolingua.com.cn

E-mail: hyjx@sinolingua.com.cn

Facebook: www.facebook.com/sinolingua

Printed by Beijing Xicheng Printing Co., Ltd.

Printed in the People's Republic of China

Unit 0

Rùmén

入 门 ··· 001

Preparation

Unit 1

Nǐ Hǎo!

你 好! ·· 031

Hello!

Unit 2

Hěn Gāoxìng Rènshi Nín!

很　高兴　认识　您! ······························· 039

Glad to Meet You!

Unit 3

Nǐ Jiā Yǒu Jǐ Kǒu Rén?

你家有几口 人? ······································ 050

How Many People Are There in Your Family?

Unit 4

Wǒ Xiǎng Qù Zhōngguó

我　想　去　中国 ·································· 060

I Want to Go to China

Unit 5

Néng Bu Néng Piányi Diǎnr?

能 不 能 便宜 点儿? ······················· 069

Can You Make It Cheaper?

Fundamental strokes

Héng   The horizontal stroke (from left to right)   Shù   The vertical stroke (from top to bottom)

Piě   The left falling stroke   Diǎn   The dot

Nà   The right falling stroke   Tí   The rising stroke

Zhé   The bending stroke   Gōu   The hook stroke

Rules of stroke order

First left, then right

First the top, then the bottom

First the horizontal, then the vertical

The outside, then the inside

Close after filling the frame

First the center, then the sides

First the main body, then join it all together

Names of some common radicals

亻	dānrénpáng	人	person, man	木	钅	jīnzìpáng	金	metal, gold	钱
彳	shuāngrénpáng		to pace	行	礻	shìzìpáng	示	to show	视
女	nǚzìpáng	女	woman	妈	衤	yīzìpáng	衣	clothes	裤
氵	sāndiǎnshuǐ	水	water	河	𧾷	zúzìpáng	足	foot	路
朩	mùzìpáng	木	tree, wood	林	马	mǎzìpáng	马（馬）	horse	骑
讠	yánzìpáng	言	words, speech	语	疒	bìngzìpáng	病	sickness	疼
口	kǒuzìpáng		mouth	吃	刂	lìdāo	刀	knife	到
饣	shízìpáng	食	to eat; food	饭	攵	fǎnwén	文	culture	教
日	rìzìpáng		sun	明	艹	cǎozìtóu		grass	茶
目	mùzìpáng		eye	眼	𥫗	zhúzìtóu	竹	bamboo	等
忄	shùxīnpáng	心	heart	忙	宀	bǎogàir		roof	寺
扌	títǔpáng	土	earth, soil	地	穴	xuébǎogàir		cave	家
扌	tíshǒupáng	手	hand	打	冖	tūbǎogàir		to cover	空
阝	zuǒ'ěrpáng	阜	hill	付	𰀪	xuézìtóu			与
阝	yòu'ěrpáng	邑	city	都	𭕄	chángzìtóu			学
孑	zǐzìpáng	子	son, child	孩	灬	sìdiǎndǐ	火	fire	常
纟	jiǎosīpáng	丝	silk	红	心	xīnzìdǐ	心	heart	点
王	wángzìpáng	玉	jade	玩	辶	zǒuzhī	走	to walk	您
车	chēzìpáng	车（車）	cart	较	囗	wéizìkuàng		enclosure	文
火	huǒzìpáng	火	fire	灯					国

Unit 0

Rùmén
入门
Preparation

0.1

▼ 汉字 Hànzì **Chinese characters**

yī	èr	sān	sì	wǔ
一	二	三	四	五
one	two	three	four	five

liù	qī	bā	jiǔ	shí
六	七	八	九	十
six	seven	eight	nine	ten

一 二 三 四 五

六 七 八 九 十

 笔 画 Bǐhuà **Strokes**

All Hànzì are composed of strokes. Here are the basic ones:

Stroke	Direction	Name	Example
一 丨 丿 丶 乁	→ ↓ ↙ ↘ ↘	Héng Shù Piě Diǎn Nà	二 十 八 六 八

There are nearly 30 kinds of strokes altogether. The other strokes are based on the basic strokes above. Here are some of them:

Stroke	Direction	Name	Example
乛 乚 乚 乙	⌐↘ ↘↙ ⌐↙↑ ⌐↙↑	Héngzhé Shùwān Shùwāngōu Héngzhéwāngōu	口 四 七 九

写 字 Xiězì **Writing**

In each of the following lines, the first character is in the Sòngtǐ form, which is the most common printed form. The second one is in the Zhèngkǎi form, which is a form used when writing with a Chinese brush (máobǐ). The third one is the form used when writing with a pen (shǒuxiětǐ).

Sòngtǐ	Zhèngkǎi	Shǒuxiětǐ	Pīnyīn	Stroke order
一	一	一	yī	一
二	二	二	èr	二 二
三	三	三	sān	三 三 三
四	四	四	sì	囗 囗 冂 四 四
五	五	五	wǔ	五 丆 五 五
六	六	六	liù	六 六 六 六
七	七	七	qī	七 七
八	八	八	bā	八 八

九　九　九　jiǔ　　丿九
十　十　十　shí　　一十

汉字知识 Hànzì Zhīshi **Points about Chinese characters**

With a history of some four thousand years, Chinese characters are one of the earliest forms of writing in the world. Chinese characters have made great contributions to the development of Chinese civilization, and are still important today.

About 60,000 Chinese characters have been used at one time or another. However, if we eliminate alternate forms and "dead" characters no longer in use, the total number of characters is between ten and twenty thousand. But even this figure is not truly representative of the number of characters that must be learned. In fact, 6,000 characters are sufficient for general reading. The characters taught here are the ones most frequently used in daily life. If you know 950 of the most frequently used characters, you will be able to recognize 90% of the characters you come across in most newspapers and magazines. If you know 3,800 characters, you will be able to recognize 99.9% of such characters.

0.2

⬇ 汉 字 Hànzì **Chinese characters**

rén	dà	kǒu	zhōng	xiǎo	shàng	xià
人	大	口	中	小	上	下
people	big	mouth	middle	small	above	below

⬇ 笔 画 Bǐhuà **Strokes**

Stroke	Direction	Name	Example
亅	↓	Shùgōu	小

⬇ 笔 顺 Bǐshùn **Stroke order**

Chinese characters should be written in the correct stroke order. This will ensure correctness, increase the speed of writing and be helpful when looking up characters in a dictionary. The main rules of stroke order are:

First left, then right	e.g. 八 八 八
First the top, then the bottom	e.g. 三 三 三 三
First the horizontal, then the vertical	e.g. 十 十 十
Enclosures before contents, and bottom enclosing stroke last	e.g. 四 四 四 四 四 四
First the center, then the sides	e.g. 小 小 小 小
First the main body, then join it all together	e.g. 中 中 中 中 中

...

The rules may appear excessively complex, but stroke order can be summed up by the first two rules: first left, then right; first the top, then the bottom.

写 字 Xiězì **Writing**

Sòngtǐ	Zhèngkǎi	Shǒuxiětǐ	Pīnyīn	Stroke order			
人	人	人	rén	丿	人		
大	大	大	dà	一	大	大	
口	口	口	kǒu	丨	口	口	
中	中	中	zhōng	丨	冂	口	中
小	小	小	xiǎo	小	小	小	
上	上	上	shàng	上	上	上	
下	下	下	xià	丅	下	下	

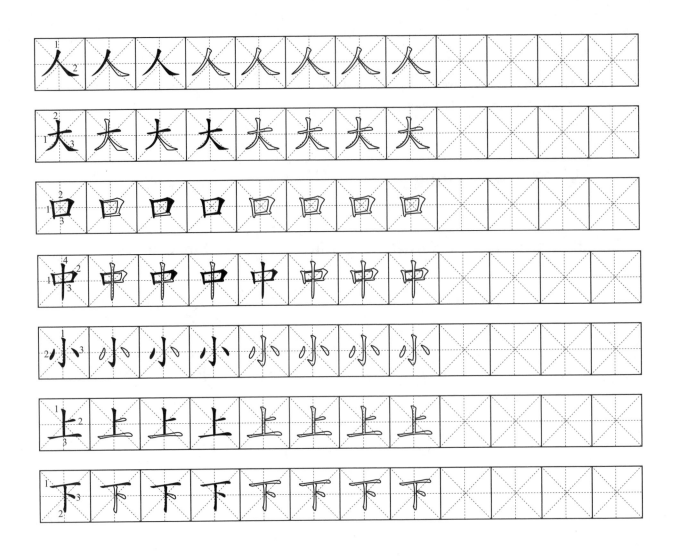

0.3

汉 字 Hànzì **Chinese characters**

guó	xué	xí	Hàn
国	学	习	汉
country	to learn	to learn	Han nationality

中国		学习	汉语
Zhōngguó		xuéxí	Hànyǔ
China		to learn, to study	Chinese language

- -

yǔ	wén	xiě	zì
语	文	写	字
words	written language	to write	character

汉语	中文		汉字
Hànyǔ	Zhōngwén		Hànzì
Chinese language	Chinese language		Chinese character

笔 画 Bǐhuà **Strokes**

Stroke	Direction	Name	Example
㇆ ㇇ ㇀ ㇈ ㇉		Héngzhégōu	刁
		Héngpiě	又
		Tí	汉、习
		Héngzhétí	语
		Hénggōu	学
		Wāngōu	学

部 件 Bùjiàn **Component**

Except for the single characters, the majority of Chinese characters can be decomposed into smaller components.

e.g.

语 = 讠（言）yán, language
+
吾 wú, I (ancient Chinese) = 五 wǔ + 口 kǒu

国 = 囗 + 玉 yù, jade

结 构 Jiégòu **Structure**

A character is more or less square in form, which is why it is called a fāngkuàizì ("square" or "block-style" character). When we put a character in a box, we must position the components properly so that it looks balanced and clear. Characters can be classified into four categories on the basis of their structure.

Structure	Shape	Percentage	Example
Single character		3%	口
Right-left structure		65%	汉
Top-bottom structure		23%	学
Enclosing structure		9%	国

写 字 Xiězì **Writing**

Sòngtǐ	Zhèngkǎi	Shǒuxiětǐ	Pīnyīn	Stroke order
国	国	国	guó	国 国 闫 闫 / 囙 国 国 国
学	学	学	xué	学 学 学 学 / 学 学 学 学
习	习	习	xí	习 习 习
汉	汉	汉	hàn	汉 汉 汉 汉 汉

语　语　语　　yǔ　　语　语　语　语
语　语　语　语

文　文　文　　wén　　文　文　文　文

写　写　写　　xiě　　写　写　写　写
写

字　字　字　　zì　　字　字　字　字
字　字

国 国 国 国 国 国 国 国 国

学 学 学 学 学 学 学 学 学

习 习 习 习 习 习 习 习 习

汉 汉 汉 汉 汉 汉 汉 汉 汉

语 语 语 语 语 语 语 语

语 语 语 语 语 语 语 语 语

文 文 文 文 文 文 文 文 文

写 写 写 写 写 写 写 写 写

字 字 字 字 字 字 字 字 字

学 字

What's the difference?

0.4

汉 字 Hànzì **Chinese characters**

nǚ	zǐ	hǎo	shuǐ	mén	wáng
女	子	好	水	门	王
female	son, child	good	water	door	king

	女子			门口	国王
	nǚzǐ			ménkǒu	guówáng
	woman			doorway	king

笔 画 Bǐhuà **Strokes**

Stroke	Direction	Name	Example
㇏	㇏	Piědiǎn	女

写 字 Xiězì **Writing**

Sòngtǐ	Zhèngkǎi	Shǒuxiětǐ	Pīnyīn	Stroke order
女	女	女	nǚ	㇛ 女 女
子	子	子	zǐ	了 了 子

好　　好　　　好　　hǎo　好　好　好　好
好　好

水　　水　　　水　　shuǐ　水　水　水　水

门　　门　　　门　　mén　门　门　门

王　　王　　　王　　wáng　王　王　王　王

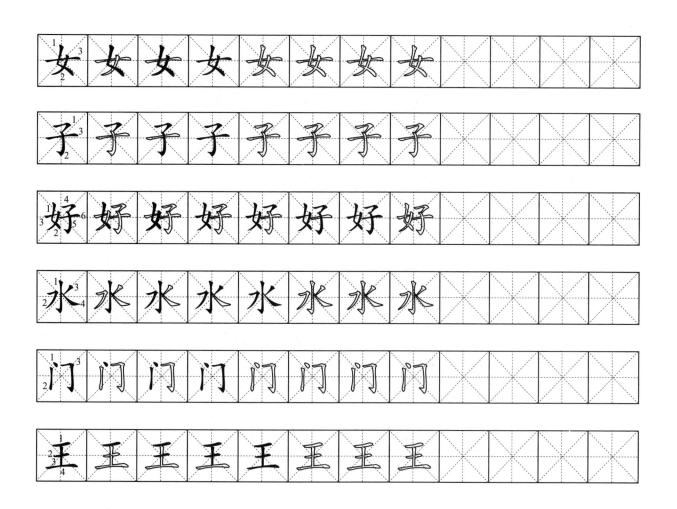

字 + 字 =? zì + zì =?

Two characters put together can frequently make a new character, e.g. 好.

Two characters put together can also make a word, e.g.

女子　nǚzǐ　woman

子女　zǐnǚ　son and daughter

好 (hǎo, good) is one character, so it can only occupy one box when writing in an exercise book. The components 女 and 子 in 好 can only occupy half the size of a box. Meanwhile 女子 (nǚzǐ, woman) form a word of two characters, 女 and 子 should each be written in a box in an exercise book.

女 子　　好

字和词 Zì Hé Cí Characters and Words

A zì can be a cí by itself, e.g. 人.

A zì can also be a component of a cí, e.g. 人口 (population, two zì but one cí).

Some frequently used characters can produce many words. e.g. 大, 人.

大人　大国　大门　大水 ……

女人

好人

小人

……

We can often guess the meaning of a word by examining its characters, e.g. 女人 "a female person, woman". But it is not always possible to do so because sometimes a word cannot be taken literally, e.g. 小人, "small / little person", actually means "a mean person, villain".

However, some zì can never be a cí in modern Chinese. They can only form cí in combination with another zì, e.g. 习 in 学习, and 语 in 汉语. They are called bound morphemes and will be marked Ⓑ in this book.

汉字知识 Hànzì Zhīshi **Points about Chinese characters**

The Evolution of Hànzì

Over the centuries, not only the forms of characters, but also their meanings, pronunciations and uses have changed to a greater or lesser extent. For example, the character 子 was not pronounced "zǐ" in ancient times and it could be used alone to refer to both sons and daughters, but now 子 (pronounced zǐ in Mandarin) is only used to make words together with other characters, e.g. 儿子, 子女, in which it only indicates sons. Furthermore, 好 originally meant "beautiful" instead of "good" as it does today.

A character may have had different pronunciations in different periods of history, and it may have very different readings in different dialects now. It is more difficult to know the ancient pronunciations than the ancient meanings of characters. We may not know how a character was pronounced, but we still can "read" the ancient literature in characters, if we have some knowledge about the ancient language. People from areas of different dialects may not be able to communicate with each other if they don't speak Mandarin (Pǔtōnghuà), but they still can understand each other by writing in characters.

0.5

汉 字 Hànzì **Chinese characters**

rì	yuè	mù	mǎ	tián
日	月	木	马	田
sun	moon	wood	horse	field

tiān	míng	lín	mā	hé
天	明	林	妈	河
sky	bright	woods	mother	river

笔 画 Bǐhuà **Strokes**

Stroke	Direction	Name	Example
𠃌		Shùzhézhégōu	马

写 字 Xiězì **Writing**

Sòngtǐ	Zhèngkǎi	Shǒuxiětǐ	Pīnyīn	Stroke order		
日	日	日	rì	丨	冂	日	日

月	月	月	yuè	月	月	月	月
木	木	木	mù	木	木	木	木
马	马	马	mǎ	马	马	马	
田	田	田	tián	田	田	田	田
天	天	天	tiān	天	天	天	天
明	明	明	míng	明 明	明 明	明 明	明 明
林	林	林	lín	林 林	林 林	林 林	林 林
妈	妈	妈	mā	妈 妈	妈 妈	妈	妈
河	河	河	hé	河 河	河 河	河 河	河 河

 汉字知识 Hànzì Zhīshi **Points about Chinese characters**

Structure of Ancient Characters

Understanding the structure of ancient Chinese characters can help us understand their origin and meaning. Most Chinese characters were formed in one of four different ways.

象形 (Xiàngxíng), pictographic. A pictographic character represents the object it refers to in a stylized form. About 5% of characters belong to this category.

 rì   sun, day

It is a pictograph of the "sun". By extension, it means "daytime" or "day".

 yuè   moon, month

It is a pictograph of the "moon".

 mù   tree, wood

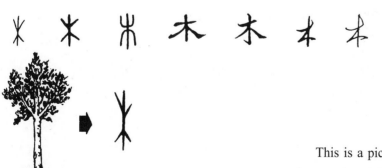

This is a pictograph of a tree with branches above and roots below.

shuǐ   water

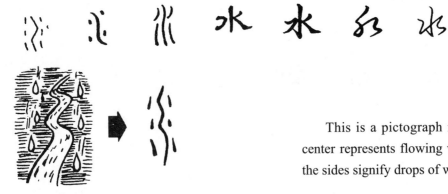

This is a pictograph in which the winding center represents flowing water, and the dots on the sides signify drops of water or waves.

 tián   field

It represents four fields.

 mǎ   horse

It is a vivid depiction of a horse.

rén   person

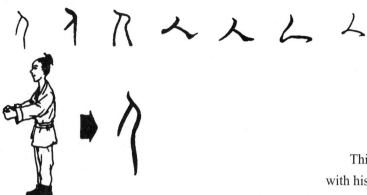

This pictograph shows a man standing
with his hands extended forward.

 kǒu   mouth

It shows a person's mouth.

 mén   door

It resembles two shutters.

zǐ   child

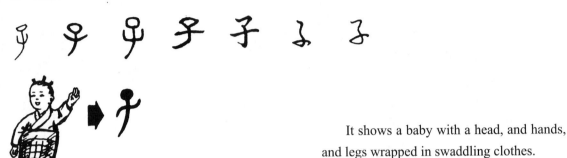

It shows a baby with a head, and hands, and legs wrapped in swaddling clothes.

 nǚ   female

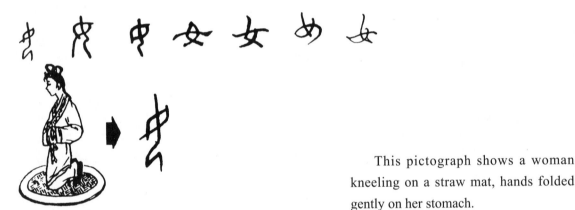

This pictograph shows a woman kneeling on a straw mat, hands folded gently on her stomach.

指事 (Zhǐshì), indicative. Indicative characters use symbols to indicate abstract meanings. There are not many characters in this category.

 shàng   above

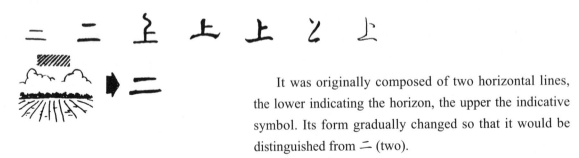

It was originally composed of two horizontal lines, the lower indicating the horizon, the upper the indicative symbol. Its form gradually changed so that it would be distinguished from 二 (two).

zhōng middle

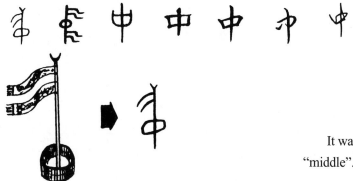

It was a flagpole with the meaning "central", "middle". Later the flag was omitted.

 xià below

It was originally composed of two horizontal lines, the upper indicating the horizon, the lower the indicative symbol. Its form gradually changed so that it would be distinguished from 二 (two).

 tiān sky, day

The originally meaning was "above the head". What is above the head is the sky, therefore it was borrowed to indicate "sky" and "the heavens".

会意 (Huìyì), associative. Associative characters result from the combination of two or more components to create a new character with a new meaning.

明	míng	bright	日 + 月
林	lín	woods	木 + 木
休	xiū	to rest	人 + 木
男	nán	male	田 + 力

形声 (Xíngshēng), picto-phonetic. A picto-phonetic character is composed of a part indicating its meaning and the other part indicating its pronunciation. Characters of this kind account for more than 80% of all Chinese characters.

妈　mā　mother　女 (picto-component) ＋ 马 (mǎ, phonetic component)

河　hé　river　水 (picto-component) ＋ 可 (kě, phonetic component)

们　men　a suffix for plural pronouns/ nouns

人 (picto-component) ＋ 门 (mén, phonetic component)

问　wèn　to ask　口 (picto-component) ＋ 门 (mén, phonetic component)

As we can see from the above examples, owing to the changes that have occurred over long periods of development in written language, phonetic components and picto-components have to a great extent lost their ability to represent pronunciation and meaning exactly.

0.6

复习汉字 (41) Fùxí Hànzì **Review (41)**

一　二　三　四　五　六　七　八　九　十

上　下　大　中　小　人　口

国　学　习　汉　语　文　写　字

女　子　好　水　门　王

日　月　木　马　田　天　明　林　妈　河

偏　旁 Piānpáng **Radicals**

The radical of a Chinese character is usually related to its meaning. If we know the names and meanings of radicals we can memorize Chinese characters more easily. The following are several common radicals:

亻	dānrénpáng	(person):	们	休
女	nǚzìpáng	(woman):	妈	好
氵	sāndiǎnshuǐ	(water):	汉	河
讠	yánzìpáng	(speech):	语	
木	mùzìpáng	(tree, wood):	林	
日	rìzìpáng	(sun):	明	

练 习 Liànxí **Exercises**

一、写出含有下列偏旁的汉字：

Write Chinese characters containing the following radicals.

亻 dānrénpáng （person） _____

女 nǚzìpáng （woman） _____

氵 sāndiǎnshuǐ （water） _____

讠 yánzìpáng （speech） _____

木 mùzìpáng （tree, wood） _____

日 rìzìpáng （sun） _____

二、在下面的汉字基础上增加笔画，把它变成另外一个汉字：

Add strokes to the following Chinese characters so that they change into other Chinese characters.

e.g. 一 ⟹ 十

人　　　大　　　口　　　十

三、补上丢失的笔画，使之成为一个汉字：

Supply the missing strokes to the following to produce Chinese characters.

上　丁　门　水　马　学　习　乙

四、学习书写自己国家的名字和自己的中文名字：

Learn to write your name and your country's name in Chinese.

五、猜一猜下面的汉字组合是什么意思：

Guess the meanings of the following combinations of Chinese characters.

好子女　　子女好

女子好　　好女子

水中月　　天上人

女人国小国王天天学习汉语口语。

汉字知识 Hànzì Zhīshi **Points about Chinese characters**

繁体字和简体字 Fántǐzì Hé Jiǎntǐzì **Traditional characters and simplified characters**

A considerable number of Chinese characters have numerous strokes and complex structures, which causes difficulties in learning, remembering and writing them. As a result, variants with fewer strokes and simpler structure have come into being over the centuries. These are known as jiǎntǐzì (simplified characters / simple form of the characters) as opposed to the original fántǐzì (traditional characters / complex form of the characters).

Chinese characters have a long history of simplification, which in fact started almost from their beginning. Simplified characters have even been found in the oracle bone inscriptions of the Shang Dynasty more than three thousand years ago. After the founding of the People's Republic of China in 1949, simplified characters already in wide currency began to be collected and standardized. In 1956 the government published Hànzì Jiǎnhuà Fāng'àn (A Scheme for Simplifying Chinese Characters), and in 1964 a further list, Jiǎnhuàzì Zǒngbiǎo (Complete List of Simplified Characters), containing a total of 2,236 simplified characters, was published.

Some examples of 繁体字(fántǐzì) and 简体字(jiǎntǐzì):

| 馬 | 媽 | 門 | 學 |
| 马 | 妈 | 门 | 学 |

| 習 | 漢 | 語 | 國 |
| 习 | 汉 | 语 | 国 |

之簡暨乎鶴林稅斬涅槃
之岸先登鳥筆記言摠持
之苑斯闕結集之侶揚其
實諦傳授之賓知其妙理
然則紹宣神典幽替玄崇
跨鷲生摩以遐籑追安什而
曾鷟可以聲融繡石采絢
雕圖則於我法師而見之

Master Daoyin's Tablet by Ouyang Tong of the Tang Dynasty

Unit 1

Nǐ Hǎo!

你 好!

Hello!

汉 字 Hànzì **Chinese characters**

- Ⓑ stands for bound morpheme.
- The figure after the character stands for the stroke number of the character.
- A star ∗ before character indicates that you are required to read it but not to write it.

1. 7 wǒ I, me

Note: The fouth stroke is Tí (from down to up), not Piě.

The original meaning was an ancient weapon. It was loaned to indicate the first person "I".

2. 7 nǐ you

你 你 你 你 你 你 你

亻 + 尔

3. 5 tā he, him

他 他 亻 他 他

亻 + 也

4. 6 tā she, her

她 她 她 如 她 她

女 + 也

5. 5 Ⓑ men plural marker for pronouns and nouns

们 们 们 们 们
イ + 门
◆ 你们　我们　他们　同学们

6. 5　jiào　to call

叫 叫 叫 叫 叫
口 + 丩
◆ 你叫什么名字？我们叫她王老师。什么叫"国王"，什么叫"王国"？

7. 4　Ⓑ　shén　what

什 什 什 什
イ + 十
◆ 什么

8. 3　Ⓑ　me　used after some Chinese characters

么 么 么
◆ 什么

9. 6　Ⓑ　míng　name

名 ク 夕 名 名 名
夕 + 口
◆ 姓名　名字

It is composed of 夕 (xī), night and 口 (kǒu), mouth. At night a person in the distance can only be distinguished if he answers to the calling of his name.

10. 9　shì　to be

是 是 是 是 是 是 是 是 是
日 + 疋
◆ 他是我同学。

The original meaning is "go along the right way". The upper part indicates something like a sundial, the lower part indicates foot.

11.* 9　nǎ　which

哪 哪 哪 哪 哪 哪 哪 哪
口 + 那
◆ 你是哪国人？

12. 4　bù　no, not

不　不　不　不

◆ 我不是英国人。我不学习英语。

13. 3　yě　also, too

力　也　也

◆ 他也不是中国人。他也学习汉语。

The original meaning was "snake".

14. 6　ma　a question mark for a yes or no questions

吗　吗　吗　吗　吗　吗

口　+　马

◆ 你是中国人吗?

15. 8　ne　a question particle

呢　呢　呢　呢　呢　呢　呢　呢

口　+　尼

◆ 我是中国人，你呢?

- -

16. 11　nín　a polite form for 你 (nǐ).

您　您　您　您　您　您　您　您　您　您

你　+　心

Note: 心(xīn), heart is added to 你 to indicate respect.

◆ 您好!

17.* 9　guì　honorable

贵　贵　贵　贵　贵　贵　贵　贵

中　+　一　+　贝

Note: 贵 originally meant "valuable". 贝(bèi) means "shell". In ancient times shells were used as money.

◆ 您贵姓?

18. 姓　8　xìng　surname

※ 姓 姓 姓 姓 姓 姓 姓

※ 女 ＋ 生

◆ 我姓王。 您贵姓？ 你姓什么？

19. 同　6 Ⓑ tóng　together, same

※ 同 同 同 同 同 同

□ 冂 ＋ 一 ＋ 口

◆ 同学

20. 老　6　lǎo　old

※ 老 老 老 老 老 老

※ 耂 ＋ 匕

◆ 老人　老师

我们的老师不老。

It shows an old man leaning on a stick.

21. 师　6 Ⓑ shī　teacher, master

※ 师 师 师 师 师 师

※ 丿 ＋ 帀

◆ 老师

22. 说　9　shuō　to say

※ 说 说 说 说 说 说 说 说 说

※ 讠 ＋ 兑

◆ 你说什么？ 我们都说汉语。

23.* 英　8 Ⓑ yīng　flower, England

※ 英 英 英 英 英 英 英 英

※ 艹 ＋ 央

Note: In ancient Chinese 英 meant "flower". Here it is the transliteration of "England" and "English".

◆ 英国　英语　英文

24.* 法　8 Ⓑ fǎ law, method, standard

法 法 法 法 法 法 法 法

氵 + 去

Note: 法 means "law" or "method". Here it is the transliteration of "France" and "French".

◆ 法国　法语　法文

25. 还　7 hái still

还 还 还 还 还 还 还

不 + 辶

◆ 还是

26. 都　10 dōu all, both

都 都 都 者 者 者 者 者 都 都

者 + 阝

◆ 我们都不是中国人。　我们都学习汉语。

27. 只　5 zhǐ only

只 只 只 只 只

◆ 她只说英语，我只说汉语。

写汉字 Xiě Hànzì **Writing**

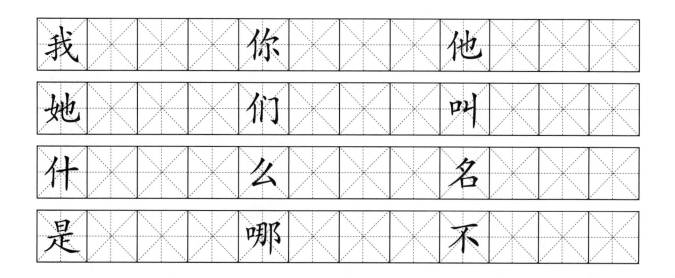

我　　你　　他
她　　们　　叫
什　　么　　名
是　　哪　　不

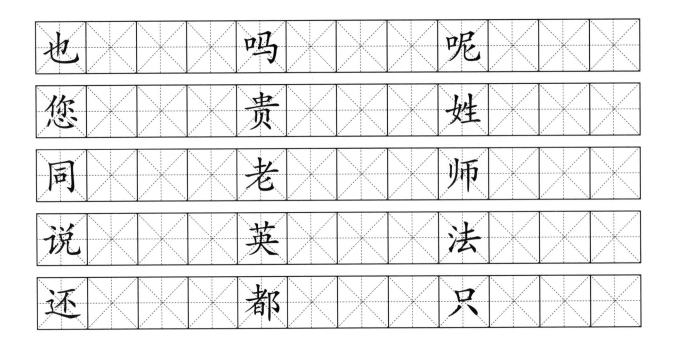

練 习 Liànxí **Exercises**

一、给下面的汉字加上一个偏旁，把它变成另外一个汉字：

Add a radical to each of the following Chinese characters to change them into other characters.

也 _____   子 _____   不 _____

你 _____   马 _____   门 _____

二、写出含有下列偏旁的汉字：

Write Chinese characters containing the following radicals.

亻 dānrénpáng（person）_____

讠 yánzìpáng （speech）_____

女 nǚzìpáng （woman）_____

口 kǒuzìpáng （mouth）_____

忄 xīnzìdǐ （heart）_____

辶 zǒuzhīdǐ （to walk）_____

三、补上丢失的笔画：

Supply the missing strokes.

我　老　名　是　都

四、组词：

Form words.

e.g.　学（学习）　学（同学）

学（　　）　　　字（　　）　　　师（　　）
同（　　）　　　语（　　）　　　还（　　）

五、看拼音写汉字：

Write the Chinese characters represented by the pinyin.

1. Nǐ jiào shénme míngzi?

2. Tā shì nǐ lǎoshī háishi nǐ tóngxué?

3. Tāmen yě xuéxí Hànyǔ.

六、猜一猜下面的句子是什么意思：

Guess the meanings of the following sentences.

1. 你说什么？

2. 你们老师老不老？

3. 我只说汉语，不说英语。

4. 同学们都说她是好老师。

汉字知识 Hànzì Zhīshi **Points about Chinese characters**

同音字 Tóngyīnzì **Homonym**

Characters which are pronounced alike, but are different in meaning and appearance like 他 and 她 are called homonyms (tóngyīnzì).

When learning a Chinese character you should remember not only the pronunciation and strokes of the character, but also its usage, i.e. what characters it combines with. Forming words is a good way to study and memorize Chinese characters. For example:

"师" shī

—— 什么 "师" ？　Shénme "shī" ?　　Which shī?

—— "老师" 的 "师"。　"Lǎoshī" de "shī".　　The Shī in lǎoshī.

Unit 2

汉字 Hànzì **Chinese characters**

1. 很　9　hěn　very

很 很 很 很 很 很 很 很 很

彳 + 艮

◆ 你很好。　我很高兴。　我很喜欢你。

2. 高　10　gāo　tall, high

高 高 高 高 高 高 高 高 高 高

◆ 他很高，我不高。

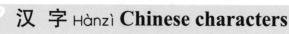
a two-story building

3. 兴　6　Ⓑ　xìng　mood

兴 兴 兴 兴 兴 兴

◆ 高兴

他很高兴，我不高兴。

4.* 认　4　Ⓑ　rèn　to recognize, to know

认 认 认 认

讠 + 人

◆ 认识

5.* 识　7　Ⓑ　shí　to recognize, to know; have a sense of

 识 识 识 识 识 识 识

✕ 讠 ＋ 只

◆ 你认识他吗？　我不认识你。

6.* 谢　12　xiè　to thank

 谢 谢 谢 谢 谢 谢 谢 谢 谢 谢 谢

✕ 讠 ＋ 身 ＋ 寸

◆ 谢谢！谢谢你！

7.　在　6　Ⓑ　zài　to be (in/on/at/...)

✕ 在 在 在 在 在

◆ 他在中国工作。

8.* 进　7　jìn　to enter; come / go in

 进 进 进 进 进 进

⬚ 井 ＋ 辶

◆ 进口

A combination of the symbol for a foot and the symbol for a cave-dwelling. 出 suggests a person leaving a dwelling.

9.* 出　5　chū　come / go out

 出 出 出 出

◆ 出口

10.* 公　4　Ⓑ　gōng　public

 公 公 公

Note: Pay attention to the difference between 么 and 公.

◆ 公司

The original meaning is "divide something equally".

11.* 司　5　Ⓑ　sī　to manage

✕ 司 司 司 司 司

Note: Pay attention to the difference between 司 and 同.

◆ 公司

12. 　3　Ⓑ　gōng　to work

※ 工　丁　工

◆ 工作　工人 worker

A wood tamper, or mallet.

13. 　7　Ⓑ　zuò　to do

※ 作　作　作　作　作　作　作

※ 亻　+　乍

◆ 工作 work, job

14. 　5　Ⓑ　kě　may, can

※ 可　可　可　可　可

◆ 可以　可是 but

15. 　4　Ⓑ　yǐ　with, by, to

※ 以　以　以　以

◆ 可以

叮 可 叮

16. 　6　hé　to join, to combine

※ 合　合　合　合　合　合

◆ 合作

17.*　9　gěi　to give

※ 给　给　给　给　给　给　给　给　给

※ 纟　+　合

◆ 你给他什么？ What will you give him?

给他打电话 telephone him

18. 　5　dǎ　to hit, to strike

※ 打　打　打　打　打

※ 扌　+　丁

Note: The third stroke is from down to up, not from up to down.

◆ 打电话 make a phone call　他打我。He hit me.

19. 电 5 Ⓑ diàn electricity

电 丨 冂 日 电

◆ 电话 phone   电脑 diànnǎo computer   电视 diànshì TV
电影 diànyǐng movie

20. 话 8 Ⓑ huà speech

话 话 话 话 话 话 话 话
讠 + 舌
◆ 说话   电话   普通话 pǔtōnghuà Putonghua   中国话

21.* 号 5 hào number

号 号 号 号 号
◆ 号码   一月一号 1ˢᵗ of January.

22.* 码 8 Ⓑ mǎ sign or thing indicating number

码 码 码 码 码 码 码 码
石 + 马
◆ 号码

23.* 发 5 fā to send

发 发 发 发 发
◆ 发电子邮件

24.* 邮 7 Ⓑ yóu to post, to mail

邮 丨 冂 由 由 由 邮
由 + 阝
◆ 邮件

25.* 件 6 Ⓑ jiàn item, piece

件 件 件 件 件 件
亻 + 牛
◆ 邮件   电子邮件

26. 8 Ⓑ de used with an adjective or attribute phrase

ϻ 的 的 的 的 的 的 的

ϻ 白 + 勺

◆ 我的电话号码 my phone number   你的工作 your work / job

----

27. 7 Ⓑ zhè this

ϻ 这 这 ㇇ 文 讠 讠 这

⬚ 文 + 辶

◆ 这是什么？   这是我的，不是你的。 It's mine, not yours.

28. 6 nà that

ϻ 习 尹 尹 那 那 那

Note: The left part of the character 那 is not 月.

◆ 那是什么？   那儿

29. 7 nán man, male

ϻ 男 男 男 男 男 男 男

✕ 田 + 力

◆ 男朋友   男同学   男老师   我们的老师是男的。

30. 8 Ⓑ péng friend

ϻ 刀 月 月 月 朋 朋 朋 朋

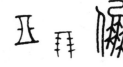

ϻ 月 + 月
◆ 朋友

A string of cowry shells. Cowry shells were used as both money and jewelry in ancient China. The form of the element 月 derives from 贝 (bèi), cowry.

31. 4 Ⓑ yǒu friend

ϻ 友 友 方 友

Note: Pay attention to the difference between 友 and 发.

◆ 朋友   友好 friendly

32. 请   10   qǐng   please

请 请 请 请 请 请 请 请 请

讠 + 青

请进！

Graphically, two people's right hands are together, signifying "friends".

33. 坐   7   zuò   to sit

坐 坐 坐 坐 坐 坐 坐

人 + 人 + 土

请坐！我坐这儿，你坐那儿。

34.* 喝   12   hē   to drink

喝 喝 喝 喝 喝 喝 喝 喝 喝 喝 喝 喝

口 + 曷

喝茶   喝水   你喝什么？

35.* 茶   9   Ⓑ   chá   tea

茶 茶 茶 茶 茶 茶 茶 茶 茶

艹 + 人 + 朩

红茶 hóngchá black tea   下午茶 xiàwǔchá afternoon tea

36. 哪   9   Ⓑ   nǎ   9   which, who, what

哪 哪 哪 哪 哪 哪 哪 哪 哪

口 + 那

哪国人   哪儿

37. 儿   2   Ⓑ   ér   r-ending retroflexion

儿 儿

这儿 here   那儿 there   哪儿 where

你在哪儿？ Where are you?

38.* 里 | 7 Ⓑ lǐ inside

米 里 里 里 里 里 里 里

◆ 这里 = 这儿　那里 = 那儿　哪里 = 哪儿

39.* 院 | 9 Ⓑ yuàn garden

米 院 院 院 院 院 院 院 院 院

米 阝 ＋ 完

◆ 学院

40.* 系 | 7 Ⓑ xì department (of a university/college)

米 系 系 系 系 系 系 系

◆ 中文系　东亚学系（东亚系）

你在什么系？

41. 怎 | 9 Ⓑ zěn how

米 怎 怎 怎 怎 怎 怎 怎 怎

米 乍 ＋ 心

◆ 怎么样　怎么 how; by what means

42. 样 | 10 Ⓑ yàng form, appearance

米 样 样 样 样 样 样 样 样 样

米 木 ＋ 羊

◆ 怎么样　一样 same　不一样 different

样儿 / 样子 appearance, shape　他什么样儿？

43. 漂 | 14 Ⓑ piào beautiful, pretty

米 漂 漂 漂 漂 漂 漂 漂 漂 漂 漂 漂 漂 漂

米 氵 ＋ 票

◆ 漂亮

44.  9 Ⓑ liàng bright

𝕄 亮 亮 亮 亮 亮 亮 亮 亮 亮

Note: Pay attention to the difference between 亮 and 高.

◆ 漂亮　明亮 bright　那儿很亮。

45.* 喜 12 Ⓑ xǐ happy event; to like

𝕄 喜 喜 喜 喜 喜 喜 喜 喜 喜 喜 喜 喜

◆ 喜欢

46.* 欢 6 Ⓑ huān joyous, merry

𝕄 欢 欢 欢 欢 欢 欢

◄ 又 ＋ 欠

◆ 喜欢

我不喜欢她那样子。I don't like her manner.

写汉字 Xiě Hànzì **Writing**

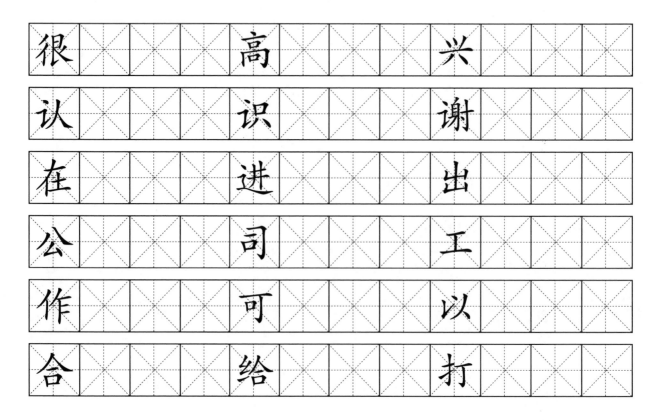

很			高			兴		
认			识			谢		
在			进			出		
公			司			工		
作			可			以		
合			给			打		

电			话			号		
码			发			邮		
件			的			这		
那			男			朋		
友			请			坐		
喝			茶			哪		
儿			里			院		
系			怎			样		
漂			亮			喜		
欢								

练 习 Liànxí Exercises

一、给下面的汉字加上一个偏旁，把它变成另外一个汉字：

Add a radical to each of the following characters to change them into other characters.

那＿＿＿＿＿＿   文＿＿＿＿＿＿   门＿＿＿＿＿＿   也＿＿＿＿＿＿

二、写出含有下列偏旁的汉字：

Write Chinese characters containing the following radicals.

扌　tíshǒupáng　　（hand）　　　＿＿＿＿＿＿＿＿＿＿＿＿＿＿

忄　xīnzìdǐ　　　（heart）　　　＿＿＿＿＿＿＿＿＿＿＿＿＿＿

木　mùzìpáng　　（tree, wood）　＿＿＿＿＿＿＿＿＿＿＿＿＿＿

讠　yánzìpáng　　（speech）　　　＿＿＿＿＿＿＿＿＿＿＿＿＿＿

氵　sāndiǎnshuǐ　（water）　　　＿＿＿＿＿＿＿＿＿＿＿＿＿＿

亻　dānrénpáng　（person）　　　＿＿＿＿＿＿＿＿＿＿＿＿＿＿

彳　shuāngrénpáng（to go; pace）＿＿＿＿＿＿＿＿＿＿＿＿＿＿

辶　zǒuzhīdǐ　　（to walk）　　＿＿＿＿＿＿＿＿＿＿＿＿＿＿

三、补上丢失的笔画：

Supply the missing strokes.

很　左　以　可　的　什　生

四、组词：

Form words.

亮（　　　　　）　　高（　　　　　）
兴（　　　　　）　　姓（　　　　　）
打（　　　　　）　　大（　　　　　）
这（　　　　　）　　还（　　　　　）
说（　　　　　）　　话（　　　　　）
学（　　　　　）　　字（　　　　　）

五、看拼音写汉字：

Write the Chinese characters represented by the pinyin.

1. Zhè shì wǒ nǚpéngyou.

2. Nǐ zài nǎr gōngzuò?

3. Nàr zěnmeyàng?

六、猜一猜下面的句子是什么意思：

Guess the meaning of the following sentences.

1. 你朋友的公司叫什么名字？

2. 我可以在这儿打电话吗？

3. 我说她很漂亮，她很高兴。

4. 你喜欢不喜欢喝中国茶？

汉字知识 Hànzì Zhīshi **Points about Chinese characters**

As we have stated before, it often happens that a Chinese character is a word, but sometimes it is only a component of a word. For example, in this text the character 高 itself is a word meaning "high" or "tall", such as 他很高 (he is tall). It can also be combined with 兴 to form the word 高兴 meaning "glad", as in 她很高兴 (she is glad). Another example is 大 (big), 大学 (university).

In Chinese there is no blank space between words. However, word units clearly exist in the minds of people. Therefore, in the sentence 我很高兴, 高兴 is always regarded as a unit of meaning.

Unit 3

Nǐ Jiā Yǒu Jǐ Kǒu Rén?

你 家 有 几 口 人?

How Many People Are There in Your Family?

汉 字 Hànzì **Chinese characters**

1.  6 dì ground, earth

地 地 地 地 地 地

土 + 也

Note: Pay attention to the difference between 他 and 地.

◆ 地方　什么地方 where　　在地上 on the ground

2. 4 ⑧ fāng square; place

方 方 方 方

◆ 地方

3. 6 yǒu have; there is

有 有 有 有 有

◆ 你家有几口人?　你有几个中国朋友?

A hand holding a piece of meat.

4. 2 jǐ how many

几 几

Note: Pay attention to the difference between 儿 and 几.

◆ 几个人

50 ▶▶

5. 3 gè used before a noun which does not have a fixed measure word of its own

个 个 个

◆ 一个人　一个地方　两个公司　三个大学

6. 10 jiā home, family

家 家 家 家 家 宀 宀 宀 家 家

A pig under a roof.

宀 ＋ 豕

◆ 我家　在家里 at home　国家 country

7. 8 bà father

爸 爸 爸 爸 爸 爸 爸 爸

父 ＋ 巴

◆ 爸爸

8. 6 xiān first

先 先 先 先 先 先

◆ 先生　张先生　我（的）先生 my husband
您先请。You first, please.
我先去。I'll go first.

A foot above a person, indicating one person going ahead of another.

9. 5 Ⓑ shēng student

生 丿 牛 生 生

◆ 学生　大学生 university student　男生　女生
中学生 middle school student　小学生 pupil

10. 4 Ⓑ tài too; greatest

太 大 大 太

◆ 你太太 your wife

Unit 3

11.* 孩 9 Ⓑ hái child

 孩 了 孩 孩 孩 孩 孩 孩 孩

◂▸ 子 + 亥

◆ 孩子 小孩子 男孩儿 女孩儿

12. 和 8 hé and

 和 和 禾 禾 和 禾 和 和

◂▸ 禾 + 口

◆ 你和我   这儿和那儿   学生和老师   小学、中学和大学

Two pieces of meat.

13. 多 6 duō many, much; a lot of

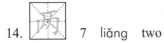 多 夕 夕 多 多 多

✗ 夕 + 夕

Note: When the upper part of 名 is reduplicated, it becomes 多.

◆ 多少   我家有很多人。   我家人很多。   你多大?

14. 两 7 liǎng two

 两 两 丙 丙 两 两 两

Note: There are two 人 inside.

◆ 两个人

15. 岁 6 suì age

 岁 岁 岁 岁 岁 岁

✗ 山 + 夕

◆ 他三十岁。

16. 爱 10 ài to love

爱 爱 爱 爱 爱 爱 爱 爱 爱 爱

爱 ⺍ + 冖 + 友

◆ 可爱　爱人 spouse

我爱她，她不爱我。

17.* 吧　7　ba　used at the end of a question

吧 吧 吧 吧 吧 吧 吧

吧 口 + 巴

◆ 她很可爱吧？你是中国人吧？

18.* 啊　10　a　used to indicate a pause or draw attention

啊 啊 啊 啊 啊 啊 啊 啊 啊 啊

啊 口 + 阝 + 可

◆ 是啊　好啊　是啊，学习汉语的人很多。

----

19. 校　10　Ⓑ　xiào　school

校 校 校 校 校 校 校 校 校 校

校 木 + 交

◆ 学校

20. 少　4　shǎo　few, little

少 少 少 少 少

Note: Pay attention to the difference between 小 and 少.

◆ 多少

我家有不少人。　我家人很少。

21* 13 Ⓑ gài generally

概 概 概 概 概 概 概 概 概 概 概 概 概

木 + 既

◆ 大概 maybe, about

22. 6 bǎi hundred

百 百 百 百 百 百

◆ 一万三千五百

23. 3 qiān thousand

千 千 千

Note: The first stroke is Piě, not Héng.

◆ 一万三千

24. 3 wàn ten thousand

万 万 万

Note: If you add a Diǎn to 万, it becomes 方 of 地方.

◆ 一万个学生

A person leaving a cave.

25. 7 méi not have

没 没 没 没 没 没 没

氵 + 几 + 又

◆ 没有

26. 13 xiǎng to think; want to do sth.

想 想 想 想 想 想 想 想 想 想 想

木 + 目 + 心

Note: There is a 心 below. Ancient people believed people thought with their 心.

◆ 让我想一下。　我想去中国。

我不想在那个公司工作。

27. 5 ràng　to let

让 让 让 让 让

讠 ＋ 上

◆ 他不让我去。He doesn't let me go there.

28. 5 qù　to go

去 去 去 去 去

◆ 你想去哪儿?

29. 7 lái　to come

来 来 来 来 来 来 来

◆ 来这儿

Its original meaning was "wheat". Later it was loaned for use in 来 (to come).

30. 4 wèi　for

为 为 为 为

◆ 你为什么不想在那个公司工作?

31. 6 ⑧ yīn　reason, cause

因 因 因 因 因 因

口 ＋ 大

◆ 因为

32. 4 fēn　branch, cent

分 分 分 分

八 ＋ 刀

◆ 分校　分公司

33. 公 4 Ⓑ gōng public

✳ 公 八 公 公

✤ 八 + 厶

Note: Pay attention to the difference between 公 and the 么 of 什么.

◆ 公司

34.* 板 8 Ⓑ bǎn board

✳ 板 板 板 板 板 板 板 板

✤ 木 + 反

◆ 老板　黑板 hēibǎn blackboard

写汉字 Xiě Hànzì **Writing**

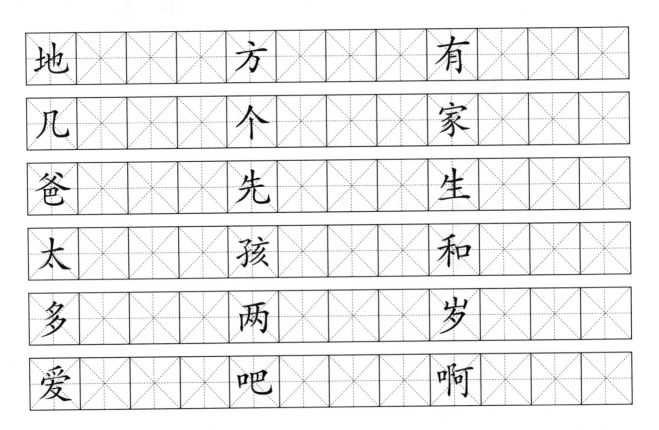

地			方			有		
几			个			家		
爸			先			生		
太			孩			和		
多			两			岁		
爱			吧			啊		

校			少			概		
百			千			万		
没			想			让		
去			来			为		
因			分			公		
板								

练 习 Liànxí **Exercises**

一、给下面的汉字换一个部首，把它变成另外一个汉字：

Change one radical of each Chinese character below to make another character.

吗 _____ 多 _____ 地 _____

二、比较下列汉字，并注上拼音：

Give the pinyin for these pairs of similar characters.

方 ( ) 万 ( ) 家 ( ) 字 ( )

名 ( ) 岁 ( ) 小 ( ) 少 ( )

姓 ( ) 生 ( ) 人 ( ) 个 ( )

三、补上丢失的笔画：

Supply the missing strokes.

为 爱 爸 冂 家 校 想

四、组词：

Form words.

地（　　　　　）　　爱（　　　　　）　　校（　　　　　）

生（　　　　　）　　没（　　　　　）　　多（　　　　　）

因（　　　　　）

五、看拼音写汉字：

Write the Chinese characters represented by the pinyin.

1. Nǐ tàitai shì shénme dìfang rén?

2. Nǐ wèi shénme xiǎng xuéxí Hànyǔ?

3. Wǒmen xuéxiào yǒu yìqiān sānbǎi gè xuésheng.

六、猜一猜下面的句子是什么意思：

Guess the meanings of the following sentences.

1. 孩子很可爱，爸爸、妈妈很爱她。

2. 他们国家人口不多，只有一千万。

3. 他很不高兴，因为他很想去那个地方工作，可是公司老板不让他去。

汉字知识 Hànzì Zhīshi Points about Chinese characters

At present, the major Chinese character input systems use keyboard input, which can be subdivided into two input techniques: one is pinyin input (Romanized spelling based on a character's pronunciation), and the other is character code input (keyboard-based codes representing Chinese character components or strokes). The pinyin input method allows input based on a character's pronunciation spelled in Hanyu pinyin, which is automatically converted into Chinese characters by the computer.

People who do not speak standard Mandarin, or who are not familiar with the pinyin system, will prefer a character code input method. The code input method selects Chinese characters by using Arabic numerals or letters of the alphabet as codes. One types in the codes, which the computer changes into characters. There must be several hundred systems for character codes, but the most widely used code system on the market today is the "five-stroke" input method.

Besides the proliferation of keyboard input methods, there has been rapid development in the field of automatic character shape recognition and voice recognition technologies. At present there are already software and peripheral products on the market that allow the computer to "recognize" a person's handwriting or voice, and convert either into Chinese characters.

Unit 4

Wǒ Xiǎng Qù Zhōngguó
我 想 去 中国
I Want to Go to China

汉 字 Hànzì **Chinese characters**

1. 图   8   tú   picture

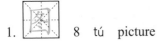 图 图 冈 冈 图 图 图

□ □ + 冬

◆ 一张图   地图

2. 张   7   zhāng   piece

 张 张 张 张 张 张

弓 + 长

◆ 一张地图   他姓张。

3. 英   8   Ⓑ   yīng   England

 英 英 英 英 英 英 英

艹 + 央

◆ 英国   英语   英文

4. 要   9   yào   to want

 要 要 要 要 要 要 要

西 + 女

◆ 你要什么？   你要干什么？

5. 3 gàn to do

✳干 干 干

Note: Pay attention to the difference between 千 and 干.

◆ 干什么

6. 9 kàn to look

✳看 看 看 看 看 看 看 看 看

✕手 + 目

◆ 看一下 看朋友 看地图 看词典 看书

7. 给 9 gěi to give; for

✳给 给 给 给 给 给 给 给 给

▷纟 + 合

◆ 给我打电话 他给我一张地图。

8. 玩 8 wán to play

✳玩 玩 玩 玩 玩 玩 玩 玩

▷王 + 元

◆ 我们去玩儿。 他不喜欢上课，只喜欢玩儿。

Unit
4

9. 知 8 Ⓑ zhī to know

✳知 知 知 知 知 知 知 知

▷矢 + 口

◆ 知道 不知道

10. 道 12 Ⓑ dào way, method

✳道 道 道 道 道 道 道 道 道 道 道

☐首 + 辶

◆ 知道

Diagram of a crossroad.

11. 6 xíng all right

❊ 行 行 行 行 行 行

❈ 彳 ＋ 丁

◆ 行。　不行。

12. 　13 Ⓑ yì　meaning, idea

❊ 意 意 意 意 意 意 意 意 意 意 意

✕ 立 ＋ 日 ＋ 心

◆ 意思

13. 　9 Ⓑ sī　to think, to consider

Two persons standing,
one in front of the other.

❊ 思 思 思 思 思 思 思 思 思

✕ 田 ＋ 心

◆ 意思

你是什么意思?　What do you mean?

他很有意思。He is interesting.

14. 　4 bǐ　to compare; than

❊ 比 比 比 比

◆ 这个比那个好。This one is better than that one.

15. 　10 Ⓑ jiào　to compare

❊ 较 较 较 较 较 较 较 较 较 较

❊ 车 ＋ 交

◆ 比较　这个比较好，那个非常好。

请比较一下这两个词。Please compare the two words.

16. 　10 zhēn　really; true

❊ 真 真 真 真 真 真 真 真 真 真

◆ 真的吗? really?　　真漂亮! It's so beautiful!

17. 　5 lóng　dragon

※ 龙 尤 尢 龙 龙

A mountain with three peaks.

18. 3 shān mountain, hill

※ 凵 山 山

◆ 小山 大山 高山

他在山上，我在山下。

----

19. 10 kè lesson

※ 课 课 课 课 课 课 课 课 课 课

※ 讠 + 果

◆ 上课 下课 有课 汉语课

课本 textbook 课文 text

20. 词 7 cí word

※ 词 词 词 词 词 词 词

※ 讠 + 司

Note: The right part is 司 of 公司.

◆ 一个词 a word 生词 new word

词典 dictionary 词语 words and expressions

21.* 典 8 Ⓑ diǎn dictionary

※ 典 只 只 典 典 典 典 典

◆ 词典 字典

22. 4 shū book

※ 书 书 书 书

◆ 一本书 看书

The roots of a tree indicated by an additional short stroke near the base of the character for 木(mù), tree.

23. 5 běn root of a plant

✳本 十 才 木 本
◆一本书　一本词典　一个本子

24.* 笔 | 10　bǐ　tool for writing or drawing

✳笔 笔 笔 笔 笔 笔 笔 笔 笔 笔
✕竹 ＋ 毛
◆这支笔你用不用？

25.* 支 | 4　zhī　measure word for long and thin objects

✳支 支 支 支
◆一支笔

26.* 教 | 11 Ⓑ　jiào teaching;　jiāo to teach

✳教 教 教 教 教 孝 孝 教 教 教
✕耂 ＋ 子 ＋ 攵
◆教 jiào 室　他教 jiāo 我们汉语。

27.* 室 | 9 Ⓑ　shì　room

✳室 室 室 室 室 室 室 室 室
✕宀 ＋ 至
◆教室　工作室

28. 问 | 6　wèn　to ask

✳问 问 问 问 问 问
◻门 ＋ 口
◆请问　他问我

29. 能 | 10　néng　can

✳能 能 能 能 能 能 能 能 能 能
◆你能不能来？

30. 用 | 5　yòng　to use

✳用 用 用 用 用

◆你用不用词典?

汉语很有用。　这本词典没（有）用 (useless)。　老板说他真没用。

31. 对　5　duì　right, correct; yes

刁　又　对　对　对

又 + 寸

◆对不对?　不对。

32. 非　8　Ⓑ　fēi　not

丨　刂　非　非　非　非　非　非

◆非常

33. 常　11　cháng　ordinary, common

常　常　常　常　常　常　常　常　常　常　常

⺌ + 口 + 巾

◆非常　常常 often

34. 谁　10　shuí, shéi　who

讠　讠　讠　讠　讠　讠　讠　谁　谁

讠 + 亻 + 主

◆他是谁?　这是谁的书?

35.* 当　6　Ⓑ　dāng　ought to

当　当　当　当　当　当

◆当然　当代 dāngdài　contemporary

36.* 然　12　Ⓑ　rán　so; correct

然　夕　夕　夕　夕　然　然　然　然　然　然

夕 + 犬 + 灬

Its original meaning was "burn".

◆当然

图				张				英			
要				干				看			
给				玩				知			
道				行				意			
思				比				较			
真				龙				山			
课				词				典			
书				本				笔			
支				教				室			
问				能				用			
对				非				常			
谁				当				然			

练 习 Liànxí **Exercises**

一、比较下列汉字，并注上拼音：

Give the pinyin for these pairs of similar characters.

干 （　　　　） 千 （　　　　） 同 （　　　　） 词 （　　　　）

木 （　　　　） 本 （　　　　） 较 （　　　　） 校 （　　　　）

问 （　　　　） 门 （　　　　）

二、补上丢失的笔画：

Supply the missing strokes.

图　妥　看　真　能　书

三、写出含有下列偏旁的汉字：

Write Chinese characters containing the following radicals.

囗　wéizìkuàng　　（enclosure）　＿＿＿＿＿＿＿＿＿＿＿＿＿＿

王　wángzìpáng　　（jade）　　　＿＿＿＿＿＿＿＿＿＿＿＿＿＿

艹　cǎozìtóu　　　（grass）　　＿＿＿＿＿＿＿＿＿＿＿＿＿＿

讠　yánzìpáng　　　（speech）　＿＿＿＿＿＿＿＿＿＿＿＿＿＿

辶　zǒuzhīdǐ　　　（to walk）　＿＿＿＿＿＿＿＿＿＿＿＿＿＿

彳　shuāngrénpáng　（to go; pace）　＿＿＿＿＿＿＿＿＿＿＿＿

四、组词：

Form words.

常 （　　　　） 比 （　　　　） 图 （　　　　）

用 （　　　　） 道 （　　　　） 课 （　　　　）

五、看拼音写汉字：

Write the Chinese characters represented by the pinyin.

1. Tā gěi wǒ yì zhāng dìtú.

2. Néng bu néng gěi wǒ kàn yíxià?

3. Zhè běn shū fēicháng yǒuyòng.

六、猜一猜下面的句子是什么意思：

Guess the meanings of the following sentences.

1. 你不问，他不说。

2. 谁知道他想要干什么！

3. 请你比较一下这两本书，哪一本有意思？

4. 这本书没有意思，可是非常有用；那本书非常有意思，可是没有用。

汉字知识 Hànzì Zhīshi **Points about Chinese characters**

There is a difference between a character dictionary (zìdiǎn) and a word dictionary (cídiǎn). Character dictionaries mainly gloss characters while word dictionaries mainly explain words. Word dictionaries can also function as character dictionaries, because they are arranged in the order of principal characters (usually the first character of a word). The principal character appears first, followed by words that begin with it. Most word dictionaries are arranged alphabetically according to the pinyin spelling of words, and usually contain a radical index, too. Some word dictionaries are arranged according to the radicals of the principal characters but also contain a pinyin index.

Unit 5

Néng Bu Néng Piányi Diǎnr?

能 不 能 便宜 点儿?

Can You Make It Cheaper?

汉 字 Hànzì **Chinese characters**

1. 商   11   Ⓑ   shāng   trade, business

◆ 商店

2. 店   8   diàn   shop

店 店 店 店 店 店 店 店

□ 广 + 占

◆ 书店   饭店   一个店 / 一家店   在店里

3.* 营   11   Ⓑ   yíng   to operate, to run

✕ 艹 + 宀 + 吕

◆ 营业   国营 state-owned

4.* 业   5   Ⓑ   yè   business

◆ 营业   工业 industry   商业 commerce, trade

5.* 员   7   Ⓑ   yuán   person, member

员 员 员 员 员 员 员

口 + 贝

6. 东　5　Ⓑ　dōng　east

东 东 东 东 东

◆ 东西　东方 the East, the Orient　东方人

7. 西　6　Ⓑ　xī　west

西 西 西 西 西 西

◆ 东西

西方 the West　西方人

8. 衣　6　Ⓑ　yī　clothes

衣 衣 衣 衣 衣 衣

◆ 衣服

It is a drawing of coat.

9. 服　8　Ⓑ　fú　clothes; to serve

服 服 服 服 服 服 服

月 + 艮

◆ 衣服

10.* 衬　8　Ⓑ　chèn　material put inside sth.

衬 衬 衬 衬 衬 衬 衬

衤 + 寸

◆ 衬衫

11.* 衫　8　Ⓑ　shān　shirt

衫 衫 衫 衫 衫 衫 衫

衤 + 彡

◆ 衬衫

12.* 裤　12　Ⓑ　kù　trousers

裤 裤 裤 裤 裤 裤 裤 裤 裤 裤

◀▶ 衤 + 库

◆ 裤子

13.* 条　7　tiáo　measure word for sth. long, narrow and thin

◀▶ 条　条　条　条　条　条　条

✕ 夂 + 朩

◆ 一条裤子　一条河

14. 会　6　huì　can; be able to

◀▶ 会　会　会　会　会　会

◆ 你会不会说汉语？

15. 买　6　mǎi　to buy

◀▶ 买　买　买　买　买　买

✕ 乛 + 头

◆ 买东西

16. 卖　8　mài　to sell

◀▶ 卖　卖　卖　卖　卖　卖　卖

✕ 士 + 头

◆ 卖东西

17.* 试　8　shì　to try

◀▶ 试　试　试　试　试　试　试

◀▶ 讠 + 式

◆ 让我试一试。/ 我来试一试。Let me try.

18. 白　5　bái　white

◀▶ 白　白　白　白　白

◆ 我要白的　白衬衫

A burning candle.

19. 红　6　hóng　red

◀▶ 红　红　红　红　红　红

◨纟 + 工

◆我要红的　红衬衫

20. 贵　9　guì　expensive, honored

◨贵 贵 贵 贵 贵 贵 贵 贵 贵

◪中 + 一 + 贝

◆这件衬衫很贵。　您贵姓？

21. 便　9 Ⓑ　pián　cheap

◨便 便 便 便 便 便 便 便

◨亻 + 更

◆便宜

22. 宜　8 Ⓑ　yí　suitable, fitting

◨宜 宜 宜 宁 宁 宜 宜 宜

◪宀 + 且

◆那儿的东西很便宜。

23. 钱　10　qián　money

◨钱 钱 钱 钱 钱 钱 钱 钱 钱 钱

◨钅 + 戋

◆多少钱　他很有钱。　我没有钱。

24.* 块　7　kuài　piece, chunk

◨块 块 块 块 坱 块 块

◨土 + 夬

◆三块钱

25. 元　4　yuán　Chinese currency unit yuan; prime, original

◨元 元 元 元

◆三元钱

26. 了　2　le　used at the end of a sentence to express an exclamation

※了　了

◆太好了！

27. 点　9　diǎn　drop, point, dot; to point, to order

※点　点　点　点　占　点　点　点　点

◆一点儿　点菜 order dishes from a menu

----

28. 饭　7　fàn　cooked rice or other cereals

※饣　饭　饭　饭　饭　饭　饭

▶饣　+　反

◆米饭　饭菜　饭店　吃饭

29.*　务　5　Ⓑ　wù　affair; be engaged in

※务　夕　务　务　务

✕夂　+　力

◆服务

30.*　菜　11　cài　dish

※一　苹　苹　苹　菜　菜　菜　菜　菜　菜　菜

✕艹　+　采

◆买菜　吃菜　中国菜

31.*　糖　16　táng　sugar

※糖　糖　糖　糖　糖　粩　粩　粩　粩　粩　糖　糖　糖　糖

▶米　+　唐

◆喜欢吃糖　糖是甜 (tián, sweet) 的。

32.*　醋　15　cù　vinegar

※醋　醋　醋　西　西　醋　醋　酐　酐　醋　醋　醋　醋　醋　醋

 酉 ＋ 昔

◆ 吃醋 be jealous (usually of a rival in love)

　　醋是酸的。

33. 鱼 8　yú　fish

　　鱼 鱼 鱼 鱼 鱼 鱼 鱼 鱼

◆ 一条鱼

34.* 酸 14　suān　sour

　　酸 酸 酸 酸 酸 酸 酸 酸 酸 酸 酸 酸 酸 酸

　　酉 ＋ 夋

◆ 这个菜比较酸。

35.* 辣 14　là　peppery, hot

　　辣 辣 辣 辣 立 辣 辣 辣 辣 辣 辣 辣 辣 辣

　　辛 ＋ 束

◆ 这个菜比较辣。

36.* 汤 6　tāng　soup

　　汤 汤 汤 汤 汤 汤

　　氵 ＋ 易

◆ 喝汤　酸辣汤

37. 牛 4　niú　cow, ox, cattle

　　牛 午 午 牛

◆ 一头牛　牛肉

The front view of an ox's head with horns.

38. 肉 6　ròu　meat

　　肉 冂 内 内 肉 肉

◆ 牛肉　鱼肉

A drawing of a piece of meat.

39.* 蔬 15　Ⓑ　shū　vegetable

⋈ 一 蔬 蔬 蔬 蔬 蔬 蔬 蔬 蔬 蔬 蔬 蔬 蔬 蔬 蔬 蔬

✕ 艹 ＋ 正 ＋ 䟱

◆ 蔬菜

40. 米   6   mǐ   rice

⋈ 米 米 米 半 米 米

◆ 大米   米饭

A scattered paddy.

41.* 饺   9   jiǎo   dumpling

⋈ 饺 饺 饺 饺 饺 饺 饺 饺 饺

⋈ 饣 ＋ 交

◆ 水饺   饺子

42.* 烧   10   shāo   to cook

⋈ 烧 烧 烧 烧 烧 烧 烧 烧 烧 烧

⋈ 火 ＋ 尧

◆ 红烧   烧菜   烧饭   烧水

43. 吃   6   chī   to eat

⋈ 吃 吃 吃 吃 吃 吃

⋈ 口 ＋ 乞

◆ 吃饭   好吃

44. 等   12   děng   to wait

⋈ 等 等 等 等 等 等 等 等 等 等 等 等

✕ 竹 ＋ 寺

◆ 请等一下。   我等你。

45. 最   12   zuì   the most

⋈ 最 最 最 最 最 最 最 最 最 最 最

✕ 日 ＋ 取

◆ 最好   最漂亮   最有意思

Unit
5

商			店			营		
业			员			东		
西			衣			服		
衬			衫			裤		
条			会			买		
卖			试			白		
红			贵			便		
宜			钱			块		
元			了			点		
饭			务			菜		
糖			醋			鱼		
酸			辣			汤		
牛			肉			蔬		

米	×	×	×	饺	×	×	×	烧	×	×	×
吃	×	×	×	等	×	×	×	最	×	×	×

练 习 Liànxí **Exercises**

一、比较下列汉字，并注上拼音：

Give the pinyin for these pairs of similar characters.

百（　　　） 白（　　　） 子（　　　） 了（　　　）

木（　　　） 本（　　　） 米（　　　） 来（　　　）

牛（　　　） 生（　　　） 西（　　　） 四（　　　）

点（　　　） 店（　　　） 买（　　　） 卖（　　　）

二、补上丢失的笔画：

Supply the missing strokes.

便　立　车　最　内　等　钱

三、写出含有下列偏旁的汉字：

Write Chinese characters containing the following radicals.

口　kǒuzìpáng　（mouth）_____

钅　jīnzìpáng　（metal）_____

饣　shízìpáng　（to eat; food）_____

纟　jiǎosīpáng　（silk）_____

⺮　zhúzìtóu　（bamboo）_____

亻　dānrénpáng　（person）_____

四、组词：

Form words.

肉（　　　） 宜（　　　） 东（　　　） 姐（　　　）

店（　　　） 先（　　　） 衣（　　　）

五、看拼音写汉字：

Write the Chinese characters represented by the pinyin.

1. Nǐ yào mǎi shénme dōngxi?

2. Wǒ xiǎng chī niúròu hé mǐfàn.

3. Tài guì le! Yǒu méiyǒu piányi yìdiǎnr de?

六、猜一猜下面的句子是什么意思：

Guess the meanings of the following sentences.

1. 请等一下，让我想一想。

2. 这家饭店的菜非常好吃，汤也很好喝。

3. 便宜的东西不好，好的东西不便宜，你说是不是？

4. 她家里有很多衣服，可是她说她没有衣服。她喜欢商店里的衣服，不喜欢家里的衣服。

汉字知识 Hànzì Zhīshi **Points about Chinese characters**

Most Chinese characters are picto-phonetic. Usually, the picto-radical is on the left and indicates the character's category of meaning, while the phonetic radical is on the right and suggests its pronunciation. For example, in the character 饭, the 饣 (shízìpáng) means that the character is related to food, and 反 indicates the pronunciation (only roughly, for 反 is in the third tone, while 饭 is fourth tone). Language and written characters have changed constantly throughout history. For example, the radical 纟 (jiǎosīpáng) of the character 红 originally referred to the color of silk products, but now 红 is used for the red color of all kinds of

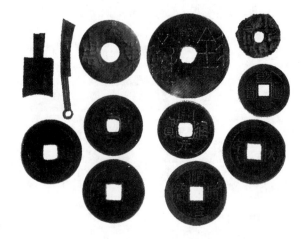

objects; the right side of the character 工 resembles the sound of 红 only in its final. The radical of 钱 is 钅 (jīnzìpáng) (gold, metal), for ancient coins were made of metal. The radical 女 (nǚzìpáng) of 姓 may refer to an earlier matrilineal society.

Unit **6** | Míngtiān Dǎsuàn Gàn Shénme?
明天 打算 干 什么？
What Are You Going to Do Tomorrow?

汉字 Hànzì **Chinese characters**

1. 4 Ⓑ jīn now, today

   今 今 今 今

   ◆ 今天

2. 6 zǎo early

   早 早 早 早 旦 早

   ✕ 日 + 十

   ◆ 早上 早饭 It's too early. 太早了！It's too early.

   早上好！Good morning.

3. 4 Ⓑ wǔ noon

   午 午 午 午

   Note: Pay attention to the difference between 午 and 牛.

   ◆ 上午 下午 中午 noon 午饭 lunch

4. 11 wǎn evening; late

   晚 晚 晚 晚 晚 晚 晚 晚 晚 晚 晚

   日 + 免

   ◆ 晚上 晚饭 太晚了。It's too late.

   他来晚了。He came late.

5. 星　9　Ⓑ　xīng　star

星 星 星 星 星 星 星 星 星

曰 + 生

◆ 星期　星星 xīngxing　star

6. 期　12　Ⓑ　qī　period

期 期 期 期 期 其 其 其 期 期 期 期

其 + 月

◆ 星期　学期 semester

7.* 算　14　suàn　to calculate

算 算 算 算 算 算 算 算 算 算 算 算 算 算

竹 + 目 + 廾

◆ 打算　算一算多少钱。

8. 约　6　yuē　to date

约 约 约 约 约 约

纟 + 勺

◆ 约会　约她在咖啡馆见面。

9. 休　6　Ⓑ　xiū　to rest

休 休 休 什 休 休

亻 + 木

◆ 休息

A person resting against a tree.

10. 息　10　Ⓑ　xī　to stop, to rest

息 息 息 息 息 息 息 息 息 息

自 + 心

◆ 休息

11. 球　11　qiú　ball

球 球 球 球 球 球 球 球 球 球 球

王 + 求

◆ 打球　地球 the earth

12.* 视　8 Ⓑ shì to look

◤ 视 礻 视 礻 视 礻 视 视

◤ 礻 + 见

Note: The left part is different from the left part of 衬 and 衫. The left part of 视 is 礻, not 衤.

◆ 电视

13. 里　7 lǐ in, inside

◤ 里 口 旦 旦 里 里 里

◆ 这里　那里　哪里

家里　学校里　商店里　教室里

14. 跟　13 gēn with, and

◤ 跟 趴 跟 趴 跟 趴 跟 趴 跟 跟 跟 跟 跟

◤ 𧾷 + 艮

◆ 跟他一起去　我跟我同学说汉语。　你跟他是什么关系?
我跟他们没有关系。

15. 起　10 Ⓑ qǐ get up

◤ 起 走 起 走 起 走 走 起 起 起

◻ 走 + 己

Note: The seventh stroke is a bit longer, in order to support 己.

◆ 一起

16. 现　8 Ⓑ xiàn now

◤ 现 现 现 现 现 现 现 现

◤ 王 + 见

◆ 现在

17. 时   7   Ⓑ   shí   time

▶️ 时 叮 町 町 町 时 时

▶️ 日 ＋ 寸

◆ 时候

18. 候   10   Ⓑ   hòu   time, season

▶️ 候 候 候 候 候 候 候 候 候 候

▶️ 亻 ＋ 丨 ＋ 癸

◆ 什么时候   有的时候 sometimes   这个时候 this moment

那个时候 that moment

他太太做饭的时候，他看电视。(……的时候，when …)

He watches TV when his wife is making dinner.

19. 钟   9   zhōng   bell, clock

▶️ 钅 钅 钅 钅 钟 钟 钟 钟 钟

▶️ 钅 ＋ 中

◆ 三点钟

20. 分   4   fēn   minute, cent

▶️ 分 分 分 分

◢◣ 八 ＋ 刀

◆ 分公司   三点四十分   五块三毛四分

21.* 刻   8   kè   quarter (of an hour)

▶️ 刻 刻 刻 亥 亥 亥 刻 刻

▶️ 亥 ＋ 刂

◆ 一点三刻

22. 半   5   bàn   half

▶️ 半 半 半 半 半

◆ 一半 half   三点半   半张地图   半天 half a day

23.* 位　7　wèi　measure word for people

位 位 位 仁 位 位 位

亻 + 立

一位朋友

24.　事　8　shì　thing

事 事 事 事 亨

亨 亨 事

Depicts catching a boar with a branch-net. The "boar" is simplified into a single stroke 一 in the modern character 事.

一件事儿　有事儿

做事儿　同事 colleague

25.　空　8　kòng　unoccupied, vacant; empty space

空 空 空 空 空 空 空

穴 + 工

有空儿　没空儿

26.　忙　6　máng　busy

忙 忙 忙 忙 忙 忙

忄 + 亡

我今天很忙。

27.* 咖　8　Ⓑ　kā　coffee

咖 咖 咖 叻 咖 咖 咖

口 + 加

咖啡

28.* 啡　11　Ⓑ　fēi　coffee

啡 啡 啡 咡 咔 啡 啡 啡 啡 啡

口 + 非

咖啡

29.* 馆　11　Ⓑ　guǎn　mansion

Ⅻ馆 馆 馆 馆 馆 馆 馆 馆 馆 馆 馆

Ⅻ饣 + 官

◆ 咖啡馆　茶馆　宾馆 bīnguǎn hotel, guesthouse

大使馆 dàshǐguǎn embassy

30. 做　11　zuò　to do

Ⅻ做 做 做 做 做 做 做 做 做 做 做

Ⅻ亻 + 故

◆ 你做什么工作？

在你们家谁做饭？

他在家里不做事儿。

31.* 功　5　Ⓑ　gōng　merit, work

Ⅻ功 功 功 功 功

Ⅻ工 + 力

◆ 功课　用功 hardworking

32. 见　4　jiàn　to see

Ⅻ见 见 见 见

◆ 见面　再见　我明天去见老师。

明天见！

一会儿见！ See you later.

Drawing of a man who opens his eyes to see.

33. 面　9　miàn　face, surface, flour, noodles

Ⅻ面 面 面 面 面 面 面 面

◆ 见面　面条 noodles

34. 关　6　Ⓑ　guān　relation

Ⅻ关 关 关 关 关 关

◆ 关系

35. 系　7　Ⓑ　xì　relation

※系 系 系 系 系 系 系 系

◆ 关系 relation

东亚（学）系 Department of East Asian Studies

36. 再 6 zài again

※再 再 丁 丙 再 再

◆ 再见！ 明天再来。 我想再去。

写汉字 Xiě Hànzì **Writing**

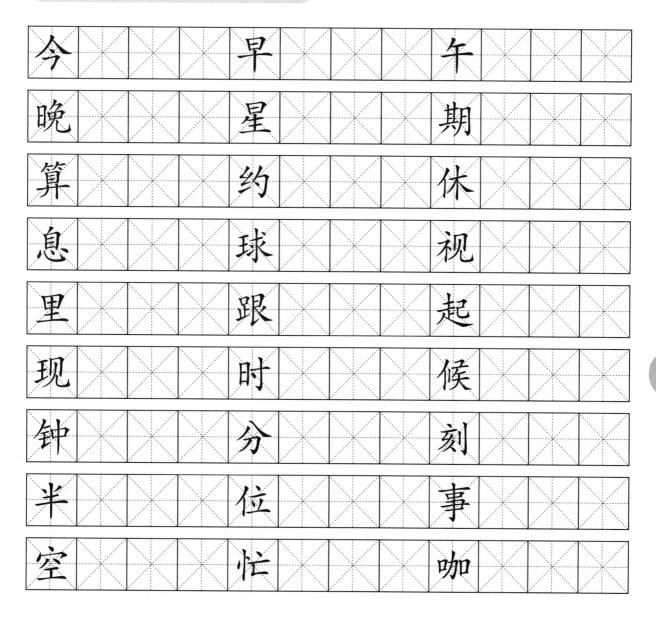

今				早				午			
晚				星				期			
算				约				休			
息				球				视			
里				跟				起			
现				时				候			
钟				分				刻			
半				位				事			
空				忙				咖			

Unit
6

啡				馆				做		
功				见				面		
关				系				再		

练 习 Liànxí **Exercises**

一、比较下列汉字，并注上拼音：

Give the pinyin for these pairs of similar characters.

红（　　　　） 约（　　　　） 来（　　　　） 半（　　　　）

今（　　　　） 会（　　　　） 午（　　　　） 牛（　　　　）

姓（　　　　） 星（　　　　） 很（　　　　） 跟（　　　　）

二、写出含有下列偏旁的汉字：

Write Chinese characters containing the following radicals.

忄　shùxīnpáng　（heart）　_____

王　wángzìpáng　（jade）　_____

𧾷　zúzìpáng　（foot）　_____

日　rìzìpáng　（sun）　_____

亻　dānrénpáng　（person）　_____

三、组词：

Form words.

休（　　　　） 期（　　　　）

起（　　　　） 面（　　　　）

再（　　　　） 关（　　　　）

现（　　　　） 早（　　　　）

四、看拼音写汉字：

Write the Chinese characters represented by the pinyin.

1. Jīntiān xīngqī jǐ?

2. Wǒmen shénme shíhou jiànmiàn?

3. Duìbuqǐ, wǒ jīntiān hěn máng, bù néng gēn nǐ yìqǐ qù dǎ qiú.

五、猜一猜下面的句子是什么意思：

Guess the meanings of the following sentences.

1. 今天晚上我有一个约会。

2. 我现在没有空，你明天上午来，行吗?

3. 休息的时候，他喜欢跟同事一起去喝咖啡。

4. 他约我明天晚上跟他见面，可是没有说在哪儿见面，只说晚上七点三刻来我家，让我在家里等他。

汉字知识 Hànzì Zhīshi **Points about Chinese characters**

多义字 Duōyìzì **Polysemous characters**

If one character is used in different words, it may have approximately the same meaning, as 工 in 工人, 工作, 打工. But sometimes the same Chinese character is used with different meanings in different words, as the 面 of 见面 and 吃面条. In these cases, 面 is called a polysemous character. Another example is the polysemous character 米. It means "rice" in the words 大米 and 米饭, while it means "meter" in 一千三百米 (here 米 is the transliteration of "meter").

"—儿"

Retroflex finals are indicated by the character 儿 in such expressions as 玩儿, 空儿. Except in the case of 这儿, 那儿 and 哪儿, one need not write retroflex endings, though they appear in the spoken language. For example, instead of 明天我有空儿 we can write 明天我有空.

Unit 7

Nǐ Shénme Shíhou Húilái?

你 什么 时候 回来?

When Will You Come Back?

汉 字 Hànzì **Chinese characters**

1. 6 nián year

丿 午 午 午 午 午 年

◆ 2013 年 一年 去年 今年 明年

A man carrying the ripe crops to his home, meaning "harvest".

2. 放 8 fàng to release, to put

放 放 放 放 放 放 放

方 + 攵

◆ 放假 放心 put one's mind at rest; rest assured

放哪儿 where to put sth.

3.* 假 11 jià holiday

假 假 假 假 假 假 假 假 假 假

亻 + 叚

◆ 放假 假日 holiday

4. 号 5 hào number

号 号 号 号 号

口 + 丂

◆ 号码 402号 一月三号

88 ▷▷

5.* 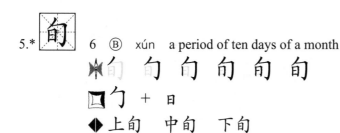 6 Ⓑ xún   a period of ten days of a month

 旬 勺 勺 旬 旬 旬

□ 勹 + 日

◆ 上旬　中旬　下旬

6. 前 9 Ⓑ qián   front

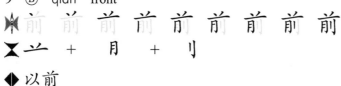 前 前 前 前 前 前 前 前

Ⓧ 丷 + 月 + 刂

◆ 以前

7. 后 6 Ⓑ hòu   behind

 后 后 后 后 后 后

◆ 以后　然后 after that; then

8. 旅 10 Ⓑ lǚ   to travel

 旅 旅 旅 旅 旅 旅 旅 旅 旅 旅

Ⓧ 方 + 良

◆ 旅行

9. 回 6 Ⓑ huí   to return

 回 口 冂 回 回 回

□ 口 + 口

◆ 回来　回去

Shows a whirlpool.

10. 担 8 Ⓑ dān   to carry, to undertake

 担 担 担 担 担 担 担 担

Ⓧ 扌 + 旦

◆ 担心

Unit 7

11. 心 4 xīn   heart

 心 心 心 心

◆ 担心　好心 good intentions　小心 careful　中心 center

12. 帮 9 bāng to help

※ 帮 帮 帮 丰 邦 邦 帮 帮

✕ 邦 + 巾

◆ 帮助

13. 助 7 Ⓑ zhù to help

※ 丿 刀 肊 肋 助 助 助

✕ 且 + 力

◆ 帮助

14. 或 8 huò or

※ 或 或 或 或 或 或 或

◆ 或者

15. 者 8 Ⓑ zhě -er, -ist

※ 者 者 者 者 者 者 者

✕ 耂 + 日

◆ 或者

16. 别 7 bié don't

※ 别 别 别 号 别 别 别

✕ 另 + 刂

◆ 你别担心

- -

17. 找 7 zhǎo look for

※ 找 找 找 找 找 找 找

✕ 扌 + 戈

Note: Pay attention to the difference between 找 and .

◆ 找东西　找人

你找谁？

18. 穿 9 chuān to wear

※ 穿 穿 穿 穿 穿 穿 穿 穿 穿

✕ 穴 + 牙

◆ 穿衣服

19.* 仔 5 Ⓑ zǎi young man; young animal

※ 仔 仔 仔 仔 仔

※ 亻 + 子

◆ 牛仔 cowboy

20.* 戴 17 dài to wear (hat, watch, gloves, glasses)

※ 戴 戴 戴 戴 戴 戴 戴 戴 戴 戴 戴 戴 戴 戴 戴 戴 戴

☐ 戈 + 田 + 共

◆ 戴眼镜

21. 眼 11 yǎn eye

※ 眼 眼 眼 眼 眼 眼 眼 眼 眼 眼 眼

※ 目 + 艮

◆ 眼镜　眼睛 eye

别眼红 don't be envious

22.* 镜 16 Ⓑ jìng mirror, lens

※ 镜 镜 镜 镜 镜 镜 镜 镜 镜 镜 镜 镜 镜 镜 镜 镜

※ 钅 + 竟

◆ 眼镜　镜子 mirror

23.* 副 11 fù measure word for a pair of things

※ 副 副 副 副 副 副 副 副 副 副 副

※ 畐 + 刂

◆ 一副眼镜

24. 头 5 tóu head

⺈ 头 头 头 头

◆ 头发

25. 发 5 Ⓑ fà hair; fā to send

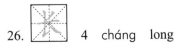 ⺄ 发 发 发 发

◆ 头发 fà 发 fā 电子邮件

26. 长 4 cháng long

 ⺄ 长 长 长

◆ 头发很长

A person with long hair.

27.* 瘦 14 shòu thin, lean

瘦 瘦 疒 疒 疒 疒 疒 疒 疒 疒 瘦 瘦 瘦 瘦

□ 疒 + 叟

◆ 他很瘦。

28. 皮 5 pí skin, peel

 皮 ⺄ 皮 皮 皮

◆ 皮肤 牛皮 苹果皮

29. 肤 6 gāng skin

 肤 肤 月 月 肝 肝 肤 肤

月 + 夫

◆ 皮肤

30. 出 5 Ⓑ chū come/go out

出 出 屮 出 出

◆ 出来 出去 出口

31. 进 7 jìn come/go in; to enter

进 进 井 井 讲 进

□ 井 + 辶

◆ 进口 进来 进去 请进！

32. 过 6 guò to cross, to pass

乂 丁 寸 寸 讨 过 过

□ 寸 + 辶

◆ 请你过一会儿再来。

33. 每 7 měi every

乂 ⺊ 仁 勹 每 每 每 每

乂 ⺈ + 母

◆ 每天 每年 每个月 每个人

34. 刚 6 gāng just

乂 刀 冂 冈 冈 刚 刚

乂 冈 + 刂

◆ 他刚回来。 他刚出去。

35.* 哦 10 ò oh

乂 吓 吓 吓 吓 吓 吓 吓 哦 哦 哦

乂 口 + 我

◆ 哦，这样子啊！

⬇ 写汉字 Xiě Hànzì **Writing**

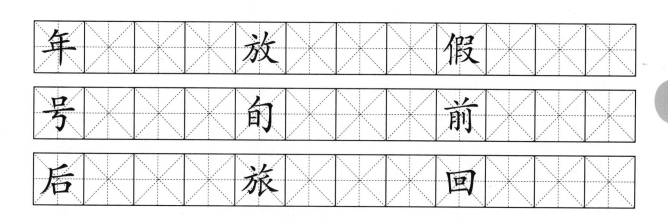

年				放				假			
号				旬				前			
后				旅				回			

Unit
7

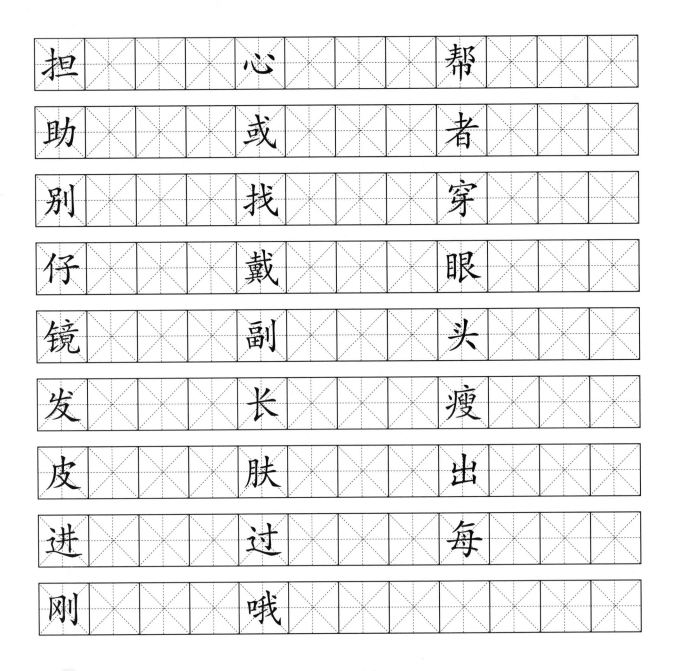

担			心			帮		
助			或			者		
别			找			穿		
仔			戴			眼		
镜			副			头		
发			长			瘦		
皮			肤			出		
进			过			每		
刚			哦					

练 习 Liànxí **Exercises**

一、比较下列汉字，并注上拼音：

Give the pinyin for these pairs of similar characters.

这（　　　）　　还（　　　）　　过（　　　）

头（　　　）　　买（　　　）　　卖（　　　）

我（　　　）　　找（　　　）　　放（　　　）　　旅（　　　）

刚（　　　）　　别（　　　）　　眼（　　　）　　跟（　　　）

者（　　　）　　都（　　　）　　长（　　　）　　张（　　　）

二、补上遗漏的笔画：

Supply the missing strokes.

发　旅　每　年　穿

三、写出含有下列偏旁的汉字：

Write Chinese characters containing the following radicals.

目　　mùzìpáng　　（eye）　　_____

扌　　tíshǒupáng　（hand）　　_____

辶　　zǒuzhīdǐ　　（to walk）　_____

心　　xīnzìdǐ　　　（heart）　　_____

四、组词：

Form words.

帮　（　　　　）　　头　（　　　　　）
以　（　　　　）　　心　（　　　　　）
或　（　　　　）　　放　（　　　　　）
担　（　　　　）　　旅　（　　　　　）

五、看拼音写汉字：

Write the Chinese characters represented by the pinyin.

1. Jīntiān jǐ yuè jǐ hào?

2. Nǐ bié dānxīn, wǒ kěyǐ bāngzhù nǐ.

3. Tā gāng chūqu, nǐ guò yíhuìr zài lái ba.

六、猜一猜下面的句子是什么意思：

Guess the meaning of the following sentences.

1. 他每天吃很多肉，可是很瘦。

2. 放假以后我打算先去打工，再用打工的钱去旅行。

3. 他六十多岁，不太高，白头发，戴一副眼镜，穿一件红衬衫。

4. 他让我进去，我让他出来。他说：“你不进来，我不出去。”我说：“你不出来，我不进去。”

⬇ 汉字知识 Hànzì Zhīshi **Points about Chinese characters**

Given the long history of Chinese characters, some Chinese characters can be written in several different ways, known as variants. For example 回 can be written in several ways: 回 囘 囬.

The standardized written form is 回. In fact, the simple forms of Chinese characters are variants which follow the rules of simplification.

Unit 8

Fùjìn Yǒu Méiyǒu Yínháng?

附近 有 没有 银行？

Is There a Bank Nearby?

 汉字 Hànzì **Chinese characters**

1. 边 5 Ⓑ biān side

 边 边 边 边 边

口力 + 辶

◆ 里边　外边　左边　前边

旁边　马路边 by the road

请这边走。 This way please.

2. 左 5 Ⓑ zuǒ left

左 左 左 左 左

◆ 左面　左边　两个月左右 two months or so

3. 右 5 Ⓑ yòu right

 右 右 右 右 右

◆ 右边　右面

4. 外 5 Ⓑ wài outside

 外 夕 夕 外 外

◆ 外面　外国　外国人　外语

5.* 附 7 Ⓑ fù to attach

Unit 8

阝 阝 阝 阝 阼 附 附

阝 + 付

◆ 附近　附件 attachment

银行在我家附近。　我家附近有一个银行。

6. 7　jìn　near

近 近 近 近 近 近 近

辶 + 斤

◆ 附近　我家离学校很近。　近视（眼）nearsighted

最近 recently

7. 10　Ⓑ　páng　beside

旁 旁 旁 旁 旁 旁 旁 旁 旁 旁

亠 + 冖 + 方

◆ 旁边　汽车在马路旁边等你们。

8. 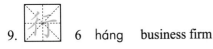 11　Ⓑ　yín　silver

钅 银 银 银 银 钅 钅 钅 银 银 银

钅 + 艮

◆ 银行　银子 silver

9. 6　háng　business firm

丿 ⼃ 彳 彳 行 行

彳 + 亍

◆ 银行　车行

10. 7　Ⓑ　yóu　to post

邮 口 曰 由 由 邮 邮

由 + 阝

◆ 邮件　邮局

11.* 局　7　jú　bureau

局 局 局 局 局 局 局

◆ 邮局

12. **路** 13 lù road

路 路 路 路 路 路 路 路 路 路 路 路

⋈ 足 + 各

◆ 马路   铁路 railway

公路 highway, road   路口 crossing

13. **走** 7 zǒu to walk, to go

走 走 走 走 走 走 走

◆ 咱们走吧! Let's go.

Drawing of a man walking and swinging his arms. The upper part 土 (tǔ) derives from the drawing of the walking man. There is a symbol of a footprint under the walking man.

14.* **拐** 8 guǎi to turn

拐 拐 拐 拐 拐 拐 拐 拐

⋈ 扌 + 另

◆ 往左拐   往右拐

15. **远** 7 yuǎn far

远 远 远 远 远 远 远

☐ 元 + 辶

◆ 我家离学校很远。   多远? How far?

16.* **离** 10 lí away from

离 离 离 离 离 离 离 离 离 离

✕ 亠 + 凶 + 内

It shows a bird being taken from a net.

◆ 这儿离市中心有多远?

现在离放假还有一个月。

17. **往** 8 wǎng toward

往 往 往 往 往 往 往 往

⋈ 彳 + 主

◆ 往前　往那边走

18. 就　12　jiù　just

就 就 就 就 就 京 京 京 京 就 就 就

京 + 尤

◆ 他就是你要找的人。　前面就是我家。

19. 客　9　Ⓑ　kè　guest

客 客 客 客 客 安 安 客 客

宀 + 各

◆ 客气

客人 guest　旅客 traveler

20. 气　4　Ⓑ　qì　gas, air

气 气 气 气

◆ 客气　天气 weather　空气 air

生气 take offense; get angry　别生我的气。

Vapor on the surface of a lake.

---

21. 公　4　Ⓑ　gōng　public

公 八 公 公

◆ 公司　公共 public

22. 共　6　Ⓑ　gòng　common; together; to share

共 共 共 共 共 共

◆ 公共

一共 (in all; altogether) 多少钱？

Two hands making an offering.

23. 汽　7　Ⓑ　qì　vapor, steam

汽 汽 汽 汽 汽 汽 汽

氵 + 气

◆ 汽车

24. 车　4　chē　vehicle

一　车　车　车　车

◆ 公共汽车　自行车

电车 tram, trolley

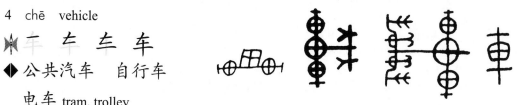

25.* 铁　10　tiě　iron

丿　铁　铁　铁　铁　铁　铁　铁　铁　铁

钅 ＋ 失

◆ 地铁　铁路 railway

26. 站　10　zhàn　station; to stand

站　站　站　站　立　站　站　站　站

立 ＋ 占

◆ 车站　站在前面　站起来 stand up

27. 自　6　Ⓑ　zì　self

自　自　冂　自　自　自

◆ 自行车　大自然 nature　自己 oneself

28. 市　5　shì　city

市　市　市　市　市

◆ 北京市　市中心 downtown

29. 骑　11　qí　ride; sit on the back of

马　马　马　马　马　骑　骑　骑　骑

马 ＋ 奇

◆ 骑马　骑自行车　骑车

30. 从　4　cóng　from

丿　从　从　从

人 ＋ 人

One person follows another.

Unit
8

101

◆ 你从哪儿来？　从来不……　never

31. 到　8　dào　until; to arrive

※到 到 到 到 到 到 到 到

▶▶至　+　刂

◆ 你到哪儿去？　从这儿到那儿

从星期一到星期五　你什么时候到学校？

32.* 换　10　huàn　to change

※换 换 换 换 换 换 换 换 换

▶▶扌　+　奂

◆ 换钱　换工作　换人　换车

33. 告　7　Ⓑ　gào　to tell

※告 告 告 告 告 告

▶▶生　+　口

◆ 告诉

34. 诉　7　Ⓑ　sù　to accuse

※诉 诉 诉 诉 诉 诉 诉

▶▶讠　+　斤

◆ 告诉

写汉字 Xiě Hànzì **Writing**

边			左			右		
外			附			近		

旁				银				行			
邮				局				路			
走				拐				远			
离				往				就			
客				气				公			
共				汽				车			
铁				站				自			
市				骑				从			
到				换				告			
诉											

练 习 Liànxí **Exercises**

一、写出含有下列部件的汉字：

Write Chinese characters containing the following components.

艮 _____   方 _____   马 _____   京 _____   走 _____

二、比较下列汉字，并注上拼音：

Give the pinyin for these pairs of similar characters.

东（　　　　）　　　车（　　　　　　）

么（　　　　）　　　公（　　　　　　）

气（　　　　）　　　汽（　　　　　　）

白（　　　　）　　　自（　　　　　　）　　百（　　　　　　）

左（　　　　）　　　右（　　　　　　）　　在（　　　　　　）

三、补上遗漏的笔画：

Supply the missing strokes.

列　就　诉　市　旁　沾

四、组词：

Form words.

告（　　　　）　　　自（　　　　　　）

气（　　　　）　　　汽（　　　　　　）

旁（　　　　）　　　外（　　　　　　）

五、看拼音写汉字：

Write the Chinese characters represented by the pinyin.

1. Wǒmen xuéxiào pángbiān yǒu yí gè yínháng.

2. Nǐ zuò gōnggòng qìchē qù háishi qí zìxíngchē qù?

3. Tā gàosu wǒ, qiánmiàn jiù shì qìchēzhàn.

六、猜一猜下面的句子是什么意思：

Guess the meanings of the following sentences.

1. 路不远，走过去就行了。

2. 银行里的人非常客气，他们从来不生气。

3. 往前走，到第三个路口往左拐，再走五六分钟，就到了。

4. 我家在市中心。我家右面有一个银行，银行旁边有一个邮局，邮局对面有一个商店，商店左面有一个饭店，我常常去那个饭店吃饭。

汉字知识 Hànzì Zhīshi **Points about Chinese characters**

多音字 Duōyīnzì **Polyphonous characters**

Some Chinese characters can be pronounced in more than one way. For example, 行 can sometimes be read xíng (as in 自行车) ; sometimes it can be read as háng (as in 银行). This kind of character is called a polyphonous character. Thus, we should first know which word the character is in before we can decide how to pronounce it.

* * * *

车 is a general character for vehicles and is contained in the following words: 火车, 汽车, 摩托车. Examples of similar characters are:

> 小学、中学、大学
> 早饭、中饭/午饭、晚饭
> 牛肉、羊肉、猪肉、鸡肉……
> 足球、篮球、排球、冰球、橄榄球、网球……
> 啤酒、葡萄酒、白酒、黄酒……

In this sense, it is easier to learn Chinese than it is to learn English. Believe it or not, there are many easier and more logical aspects of Chinese than in other languages, e.g. the numerals, that you will gradually learn in the course of your Chinese study.

Hànzì Suǒyǐn
汉字索引
Index of Chinese Characters

72. 共 gòng / 8	100. 家 jiā / 3	129. 里 lǐ * / 2
73. 拐 guǎi * / 8	101. 假 jiǎ * / 7	里 lǐ / 6
74. 关 guān / 6	102. 见 jiàn / 6	130. 两 liǎng / 3
75. 馆 guǎn * / 6	103. 件 jiàn * / 2	131. 亮 liàng / 2
76. 贵 guì * / 1	104. 饺 jiǎo * / 5	132. 了 le / 5
贵 guì / 5	105. 叫 jiào / 1	133. 林 lín / 0
77. 国 guó / 0	106. 较 jiào / 4	134. 六 liù / 0
78. 过 guò / 7	107. 教 jiāo, jiào * / 4	135. 龙 lóng / 4
79. 还 hái / 1	108. 今 jīn / 6	136. 路 lù / 8
80. 孩 hái * / 3	109. 近 jìn / 8	137. 旅 lǚ / 7
81. 汉 hàn / 0	110. 进 jìn * / 2	138. 妈 mā / 0
82. 行 háng / 4	进 jìn / 7	139. 马 mǎ / 0
83. 好 hǎo / 0	111. 镜 jìng * / 7	140. 码 mǎ * / 2
84. 号 hào * / 2	112. 九 jiǔ / 0	141. 吗 ma / 1
号 hào / 7	113. 就 jiù / 8	142. 买 mǎi / 5
85. 喝 hē * / 2	114. 局 jú * / 8	143. 卖 mài / 5
86. 合 hé / 2	115. 咖 kā * / 6	144. 忙 máng / 6
87. 和 hé / 3	116. 看 kàn / 4	145. 么 me / 1
88. 河 hé / 0	117. 可 kě / 2	146. 没 méi / 3
89. 很 hěn / 2	118. 刻 kè * / 6	147. 每 měi / 7
90. 红 hóng / 5	119. 客 kè / 8	148. 门 mén / 0
91. 后 hòu / 7	120. 课 kè / 4	149. 们 men / 1
92. 候 hòu / 6	121. 空 kōng / 6	150. 米 mǐ / 5
93. 话 huà / 2	122. 口 kǒu / 0	151. 面 miàn / 6
94. 欢 huān * / 2	123. 裤 kù * / 5	152. 名 míng / 1
95. 换 huàn * / 8	124. 块 kuài * / 5	153. 明 míng / 0
96. 回 huí / 7	125. 辣 là * / 5	154. 木 mù / 0
97. 会 huì / 5	126. 来 lái / 3	155. 哪 nǎ * / 1
98. 或 huò / 7	127. 老 lǎo / 1	哪 nǎ / 2
99. 几 jǐ / 3	128. 离 lí * / 8	156. 那 nà / 2

157. 男 nán / 2

158. 呢 ne / 1

159. 能 néng / 4

160. 你 nǐ / 1

161. 年 nián / 7

162. 您 nín / 1

163. 牛 niú / 5

164. 女 nǚ / 0

165. 哦 è * / 7

166. 旁 páng / 8

167. 朋 péng / 2

168. 皮 pí / 7

169. 便 pián / 5

170. 漂 piāo / 2

171. 七 qī / 0

172. 期 qī / 6

173. 骑 qí / 8

174. 起 qǐ / 6

175. 气 qì / 8

176. 汽 qì / 8

177. 千 qiān / 3

178. 前 qián / 7

179. 钱 qián / 5

180. 请 qǐng / 2

181. 球 qiú / 6

182. 去 qù / 3

183. 然 rán * / 4

184. 让 ràng / 3

185. 人 rén / 0

186. 认 rèn * / 2

187. 日 rì / 0

188. 肉 ròu / 5

189. 三 sān / 0

190. 山 shān / 4

191. 衫 shān * / 5

192. 商 shāng / 5

193. 上 shàng / 0

194. 烧 shāo * / 5

195. 少 shǎo / 3

196. 生 shēng / 3

197. 师 shī / 1

198. 十 shí / 0

199. 什 shén / 1

200. 时 shí / 6

201. 识 shí * / 2

202. 市 shì / 8

203. 事 shì / 6

204. 视 shì * / 6

205. 试 shì * / 5

206. 室 shì * / 4

207. 是 shì / 1

208. 瘦 shòu * / 7

209. 书 shū / 4

210. 蔬 shū * / 5

211. 谁 shéi, shuí / 4

212. 水 shuǐ / 0

213. 说 shuō / 1

214. 司 sī * / 2

215. 思 sī / 4

216. 四 sì / 0

217. 诉 sù / 8

218. 酸 suān * / 5

219. 算 suàn * / 6

220. 岁 suì / 3

221. 他 tā / 1

222. 她 tā / 1

223. 太 tài / 3

224. 汤 tāng * / 5

225. 糖 táng * / 5

226. 天 tiān / 0

227. 田 tián / 0

228. 条 tiáo * / 5

229. 铁 tiě * / 8

230. 同 tóng / 1

231. 头 tóu / 7

232. 图 tú / 4

233. 外 wài / 8

234. 玩 wán / 4

235. 晚 wǎn / 6

236. 万 wàn / 3

237. 王 wáng / 0

238. 往 wǎng / 8

239. 为 wèi / 3

240. 位 wèi * / 6

241. 文 wén / 0

242. 问 wèn / 4

243. 我 wǒ / 1

244. 五 wǔ / 0

245. 午 wǔ / 6

246. 务 wù * / 5

247. 西 xī / 5

248. 息 xī / 6

249. 习 xí / 0

250. 喜 xǐ * / 2

251. 系 xì * / 2
　　　系 xì / 6

252. 下 xià / 0

253. 先 xiān / 3

254. 现 xiàn / 6

255. 想 xiǎng / 3

256. 小 xiǎo / 0

257. 校 xiào / 3

258. 写 xiě / 0

259. 谢 xiè * / 2

260. 心 xīn / 7

261. 兴 xīng / 2

262. 星 xīng / 6

263. 行 xíng / 8

264. 姓 xìng / 1

265. 休 xiū / 6

266. 学 xué / 0

267. 旬 xún * / 7

268. 眼 yǎn / 7

269. 样 yàng / 2

270. 要 yào / 4

271. 也 yě / 1

272. 业 yè * / 5

273. 一 yī / 0

274. 衣 yī / 5

275. 宜 yí / 5

276. 以 yǐ / 2

277. 意 yì / 4

278. 因 yīn / 3

279. 银 yín / 8

280. 英 yīng * / 1
　　　英 yīng / 4

281. 营 yíng * / 5

282. 用 yòng / 4

283. 邮 yóu * / 2
　　　邮 yóu / 8

284. 友 yǒu / 2

285. 有 yǒu / 3

286. 右 yòu / 8

287. 鱼 yú / 5

288. 语 yǔ / 0

289. 元 yuán / 5

290. 员 yuán * / 5

291. 远 yuǎn / 8

292. 院 yuàn * / 2

293. 约 yuē / 6

294. 月 yuè / 0

295. 再 zài / 6

296. 在 zài / 2

297. 早 zǎo / 6

298. 怎 zěn / 2

299. 站 zhàn / 8

300. 张 zhāng / 4

301. 找 zhǎo / 7

302. 者 zhě / 7

303. 这 zhè / 2

304. 真 zhēn / 4

305. 支 zhī * / 4

306. 知 zhī / 4

307. 只 zhī / 1

308. 中 zhōng / 0

309. 钟 zhōng / 6

310. 助 zhù / 7

311. 子 zǐ / 0

312. 仔 zǐ * / 7

313. 字 zì / 0

314. 自 zì / 8

315. 走 zǒu / 8

316. 最 zuì / 5

317. 左 zuǒ / 8

318. 作 zuò / 2

319. 坐 zuò / 2

320. 做 zuò / 6

Liànxí Cānkǎo Dá'àn
练习参考答案
Key to Exercises

Unit 0

一、(单人旁) 们　休

　　(女字旁) 好　妈

　　(三点水) 汉　河

　　(言字旁) 语

　　(木字旁) 林

　　(日字旁) 明

二、大　天　中　木

三、上　下　门　水　马　学　习　九

Unit 1

一、(也) 他　她　　(子) 好　字　学

　　(不) 还　　　　(你) 您

　　(马) 吗　妈　　(门) 们

二、(单人旁) 你　们　他　什

　　(言字旁) 语　说

　　(女字旁) 好　妈　她　姓

　　(口字旁) 吗　呢　叫　哪

　　(心字底) 您

　　(走之底) 还

三、我　老　名　是　都

四、学 (学习、同学)　字 (名字、汉字)

　　师 (老师)　同 (同学)

　　语 (汉语、英语、法语)　还 (还是)

五、1. 你叫什么名字?

　　2. 他是你老师还是你同学?

3. 他们也学习汉语。

Unit 2

一、(那) 哪　　(文) 这　　(门) 们

　　(也) 他　她

二、(提手旁) 打

　　(心字底) 怎　您

　　(木字旁) 样

　　(言字旁) 认　识　话　请　谢　说　语

　　(三点水) 漂　汉　河

　　(单人旁) 他　你　件　们　什

　　(双人旁) 很

　　(走之底) 进　这　还

三、很　在　以　可　的　作　坐

四、亮 (漂亮、明亮)　高 (高兴)

　　兴 (高兴)　姓 (姓名、贵姓)

　　打 (打电话)　大 (大学)

　　这 (这儿、这里)　还 (还是)

　　说 (说汉语、说话)　话 (电话、中国话)

　　学 (学习)　字 (汉字、名字、写字)

五、1. 这是我女朋友。

　　2. 你在哪儿工作?

　　3. 那儿怎么样?

Unit 3

一、(吗) 妈　(多) 名　(地) 他　她

二、方（fāng）　　万（wàn）
　　家（jiā）　　字（zì）
　　名（míng）　　岁（suì）
　　小（xiǎo）　　少（shǎo）
　　姓（xìng）　　生（shēng）
　　人（rén）　　个（gè）

三、为 爱 爸 两 家 校 想

四、地（地方）　爱（可爱、爱人）
　　校（学校）　生（学生）
　　没（没有）　多（多少）
　　因（因为）

五、1. 你太太是什么地方人？
　　2. 你为什么想学习汉语？
　　3. 我们学校有一千三百个学生。

Unit 4

一、干（gàn）　　千（qiān）
　　同（tóng）　　词（cí）
　　木（mù）　　本（běn）
　　较（jiào）　　校（xiào）
　　问（wèn）　　门（mén）

二、图 要 看 真 能 书

三、（围字框）图 国
　　（王字旁）玩
　　（草字头）茶 英
　　（言字旁）谁 课 词 说 话 语 请
　　（走之底）这 还 道
　　（双人旁）行 很

四、常（非常、常常）
　　比（比较）　　图（地图）
　　用（有用）　　道（知道）

课（上课、下课、课本、课文）

五、1. 他给我一张地图。
　　2. 能不能给我看一下？
　　3. 这本书非常有用。

Unit 5

一、百（bǎi）　　白（bái）
　　子（zǐ）　　了（le）
　　木（mù）　　本（běn）
　　米（mǐ）　　来（lái）
　　牛（niú）　　生（shēng）
　　西（xī）　　四（sì）
　　点（diǎn）　　店（diàn）
　　买（mǎi）　　卖（mài）

二、便 宜 东 最 肉 等 钱

三、（口字旁）吃 喝 吗 呢 哪 吧 叫
　　（金字旁）钱
　　（食字旁）饭
　　（绞丝旁）红 给
　　（竹字头）等 笔
　　（单人旁）件 便 作

四、肉（牛肉）　宜（便宜）　东（东西）
　　姐（小姐、姐姐）　店（饭店、商店）
　　先（先生）　衣（衣服）

五、1. 你要买什么东西？
　　2. 我想吃牛肉和米饭。
　　3. 太贵了！有没有便宜一点儿的？

Unit 6

一、红（hóng）　　约（yuē）
　　来（lái）　　半（bàn）
　　今（jīn）　　会（huì）

午（wǔ）　　　　牛（niú）

姓（xìng）　　　星（xīng）

很（hěn）　　　跟（gēn）

二、（竖心旁）忙

　　（王字旁）现　球　玩

　　（足字旁）跟

　　（日字旁）时　明　晚

　　（单人旁）休　做　候　位　作　件　便

三、休（休息）　期（星期、学期）

　　起（一起）　面（见面、里面）

　　再（再见）　关（关系）

　　现（现在）　早（早上）

四、1. 今天星期几？

　　2. 我们什么时候见面？

　　3. 对不起，我今天很忙，不能跟你一
　　　起去打球。

Unit 7

一、这（zhè）　还（hái）　过（guò）

　　头（tóu）　买（mǎi）　卖（mài）

　　我（wǒ）　找（zhǎo）

　　放（fàng）　旅（lǚ）

　　刚（gāng）　别（bié）

　　眼（yǎn）　跟（gēn）

　　者（zhě）　都（dōu）

　　长（cháng）　张（zhāng）

二、发　旅　每　年　穿

三、（目字旁）眼

　　（提手旁）找　担　打　接

　　（走之底）过　进　还　这　道

　　（心字底）您　怎　意　思　想　息

四、帮（帮助）　头（头发）

　　以（可以、以后、以前）

　　心（担心、放心、小心、真心、好心、
　　　心意、点心）

　　或（或者）　放（放假、放心）

　　担（担心）　旅（旅行）

五、1. 今天几月几号？

　　2. 你别担心，我可以帮助你。

　　3. 他刚出去，你过一会儿再来吧。

Unit 8

一、（艮）很　跟　银　眼

　　（方）放　旅　旁

　　（马）吗　妈　码　骑

　　（京）就

　　（走）起

二、东（dōng）　车（chē）

　　么（me）　公（gōng）

　　气（qì）　汽（qì）

　　白（bái）　自（zì）　百（bǎi）

　　左（zuǒ）　右（yòu）　在（zài）

三、到　就　诉　市　旁　站

四、告（告诉）　自（自行车）

　　气（客气、天气、生气）　汽（汽车）

　　旁（旁边）　外（外面、外国、外语）

五、1. 我们学校旁边有一个银行。

　　2. 你坐公共汽车去还是骑自行车去？

　　3. 他告诉我，前面就是汽车站。

责任编辑：陆 瑜
英文编辑：薛彧威 范逊敏
封面设计：Daniel Gutierrez
插 图：笑 龙

图书在版编目（CIP）数据

《当代中文》汉字本 . 1 / 吴中伟主编 . —修订版 . —北京：华语教学出版社，2014
ISBN 978-7-5138-0619-0

Ⅰ . ①当… Ⅱ . ①吴… Ⅲ . ①汉语 – 对外汉语教学 – 教学参考资料 Ⅳ . ① H195.4

中国版本图书馆 CIP 数据核字 (2013) 第 297879 号

《当代中文》修订版
汉字本
1
主编 吴中伟
*

© 华语教学出版社有限责任公司
华语教学出版社有限责任公司出版
（中国北京百万庄大街 24 号 邮政编码 100037）
电话：(86)10-68320585, 68997826
传真：(86)10-68997826, 68326333
网址：www.sinolingua.com.cn
电子信箱：hyjx@sinolingua.com.cn
新浪微博地址：http://weibo.com/sinolinguavip
北京玺诚印务有限公司印刷
2003 年（16 开）第 1 版
2014 年（16 开）第 2 版
2020 年第 2 版第 6 次印刷
（汉英）
ISBN 978-7-5138-0619-0
004500